Metaphor / *Terence Hawkes*

Methuen

LONDON and NEW YORK

First published 1972
by Methuen & Co. Ltd
11 New Fetter Lane, London EC4P 4EE
Reprinted twice
Reprinted with revised bibliography 1984
Reprinted 1986

Published in the USA by
Methuen & Co.
in association with Methuen, Inc.
29 West 35th Street, New York, NY 10001

© 1972 Terence Hawkes

Printed in Great Britain
by J. W. Arrowsmith Ltd, Bristol

ISBN 0 416 09030 3

to ANN

Contents

Founder Editor's Preface

The volumes composing the Critical Idiom deal with a wide variety of key terms in our critical vocabulary. The purpose of the series differs from that served by the standard glossaries of literary terms. Many terms are adequately defined for the needs of students by the brief entries in these glossaries, and such terms do not call for attention in the present series. But there are other terms which cannot be made familiar by means of compact definitions. Students need to grow accustomed to them through simple and straightforward but reasonably full discussions. The main purpose of this series is to provide such discussions.

Many critics have borrowed methods and criteria from currently influential bodies of knowledge or belief that have developed without particular reference to literature. In our own century, some of them have drawn on art-history, psychology, or sociology. Others, strong in a comprehensive faith, have looked at literature and literary criticism from a Marxist or a Christian or some other sharply defined point of view. The result has been the importation into literary criticism of terms from the vocabularies of these sciences and creeds. Discussions of such bodies of knowledge and belief in their bearing upon literature and literary criticism form a natural extension of the initial aim of the Critical Idiom.

Because of their diversity of subject-matter, the studies in the series vary considerably in structure. But all authors have tried to give as full illustrative quotation as possible, to make reference whenever appropriate to more than one literature, and to write in such a way as to guide readers towards the short bibliographies in which they have made suggestions for further reading.

University of Manchester   John D. Jump

Acknowledgements

I should like to thank Professor John D. Jump for his encouragement over a long period. Also several of my colleagues at University College, Cardiff kindly listened to or read sections of this material and made extremely helpful comments on it: in particular Nick Fisher of the Department of Classics, and G. Ingli James, Peter Garside and Robin Moffat of the Department of English. They will know that I am grateful to them.

A large portion of this book was written whilst I was in the United States in the summer of 1971, as a visiting professor at Rutgers University. My thanks must go to Professor Maurice Charney and his wife Hanna, whose kindly acumen and dazzling hospitality deserve a better relic, and to Professor Daniel Howard whose benevolence made my trip possible. The friendship of Louis and Joan Slovinsky and of Bob and Arlene Trudell proved powerfully sustaining. My greatest debt of gratitude remains, as ever, to my wife.

Finally, I must thank my argumentative students who will be the first to recognize the extent to which, over the years, I have become the vehicle to their tenor.

T.H.

I

Metaphor and Figurative Language

> The degrees of metaphor. The absolute object
> slightly turned is a metaphor of the object
>
> (Wallace Stevens)

The word *metaphor* comes from the Greek word *metaphora* derived from *meta* meaning 'over', and *pherein*, 'to carry'. It refers to a particular set of linguistic processes whereby aspects of one object are 'carried over' or transferred to another object, so that the second object is spoken of as if it were the first. There are various types of metaphor, and the number of 'objects' involved can vary, but the general procedure of 'transference' remains the same:

> Awake! for Morning in the Bowl of Night
> Has flung the stone that puts the stars to flight.
>
> (Edward FitzGerald, *The Rubáiyát of Omar Khayyám*)

> L'homme n'a point de port, le temps n'a point de rive:
> Il coule, et nous passons!
>
> (Alphonse de Lamartine, *Le Lac*)

> It's what's under the bonnet that counts!
>
> (Car advertisement)

Metaphor is traditionally taken to be the most fundamental form of figurative language.

Figurative language is language which doesn't mean what it says. Cars do not wear bonnets. Men are not ships. Time is not a river. Night is not a bowl of water, and Morning does not throw stones into it.

Language which means (or intends to mean) what it says, and which uses words in their 'standard' sense, derived from the common practice of ordinary speakers of the language, is said to be *literal*. Figurative language deliberately *interferes* with the system of literal usage by its assumption that terms literally connected with one object can be transferred to another object. The *interference* takes the form of *transference*, or 'carrying over', with the aim of achieving a new, wider, 'special' or more precise meaning.

Inevitably, figurative language is usually descriptive, and the transferences involved result in what seem to be 'pictures' or 'images':

> An aged man is but a paltry thing,
> A tattered coat upon a stick ...
> (W. B. Yeats, *Sailing to Byzantium*)

However, the term 'imagery' is essentially misleading when it is used to refer to figurative language, because it presupposes that its primary appeal is to the eye. This is not the case. The appeal of figurative language may include the visual sense, as the above metaphor certainly shows, but its essential mode is *linguistic* and as a result its appeal goes much further. In this case an extensive non-visual response involving myth and symbol in terms of the relationship of birds and scarecrows is required.

The various forms of 'transference' are called *figures of speech* or *tropes*; that is, 'turnings' of language away from literal meanings and towards figurative meanings. Metaphor is generally considered to manifest the basic pattern of transference involved and so can be thought of as the fundamental 'figure' of speech. The other figures tend to be versions of metaphor's prototype, particularly the three main traditional categories:

(a) *Simile*. Where metaphor assumes that the transference is possible or has already taken place ('the bonnet of the car'), simile *proposes* the transference, and *explains* it by means of terms such as 'like' or 'as if': 'this piece of steel covers the car's engine as if it were a bonnet covering a woman's head', or,

> I walked abroad
> And saw the ruddy moon lean over a hedge
> Like a red-faced farmer.
>
> (T. E. Hulme, *Autumn*)

In general, because of its 'like' or 'as if' structure, simile involves a more visually inclined relationship between its elements than metaphor. In fact, it is sometimes assumed that simile is metaphor's poor relation, offering only the 'bare bones' of the transferring process in the form of a limited analogy or comparison, whose 'range' is narrow, because pre-determined.

On the contrary, the 'controlled' effects of simile can be as great or greater than the wider but often vaguer implications of metaphor. In any case, abstract value-judgements are pointless. In the following lines it would be difficult to say whether the metaphors or the similes were the more effective:

> The yellow fog that rubs its back upon the window-panes,
> The yellow smoke that rubs its muzzle on the window panes
> Licked its tongue into the corners of the evening . . .
>
> (T. S. Eliot, *The Love Song of J. Alfred Prufrock*)

> Voici le soir charmant, ami du criminel;
> Il vient comme un complice, à pas de loup; le ciel
> Se ferme lentement comme une grande alcôve,
> Et l'homme impatient se change en bête fauve.
>
> (Baudelaire, *Le Crépuscule du soir*)

> It is a beauteous evening, calm and free,
> The holy time is quiet as a Nun
> Breathless with adoration . . .
>
> (Wordsworth, *Sonnets*)

(b) *Synecdoche*. The word is Greek, derived from *synekdechesthai* meaning 'to receive jointly'. Here the transference takes the form of a part of something being 'carried over' to stand in place of the whole thing, or vice versa. 'Twenty *summers*' for twenty years; 'ten *hands*' for ten men; or, in Milton's *Lycidas*, 'blind *mouths*' for the corrupt priests.

(c) *Metonymy*. This word comes from the Greek word *metonymia*, derived from *meta* 'change' and *onoma* 'name'. Here the name of a thing is transferred to take the place of something else with which it is associated: 'The White House' for the President of the United States; 'The Crown' for the Monarch and so on. Clearly the process also involves *personification*, and is closely related to that of *synecdoche*. The Old English form of transference known as the *Kenning* involves the substitution of part for whole, as in 'the whale's way' for the sea, and so could also be placed in this category.

Of course it would be possible greatly to extend and complicate the list of these categories, and traditional rhetoric has traditionally done so. But it is doubtful whether much is gained from this when it comes to the practical *application* of them to works of literature. The distinctions between the various categories become so finely drawn – we can see this already beginning to happen even in the case of metonymy and synecdoche – and so difficult to remember, that it becomes almost impossible to use them without a kind of simple-minded 'reduction' of the work they are intended to illuminate. Something in the mind withers at the prospect of unfolding the mysteries of Antonomasia, Hyperbaton, Metalepsis and the rest, and in any case these categories were designed principally as standard formulae to help with *composition*, not critical response. Much of the mystery seems to disappear once the basic formal and linguistic principle of transference is seen either to animate all of them, or to be what they describe. They are types of Metaphor.

On the other hand, 'Metaphor' only exists because metaphors do. And metaphors only exist when they actually occur in language, in society, and in time. None of these elements is a constant factor. In other words, the notion of metaphor itself is shaped at any given time by linguistic and social pressures, as well as by its own history: it has no pristine form.

Given this, the most fruitful way of approaching the topic seems to be through an examination of the metaphorical process itself by means of an account of the *idea* of metaphor as a *social* and *historical* phenomenon deriving from attitudes towards language. We may hope that these terms will come, in the end, to illuminate each other; that an enlarging metaphorical 'transference' may take place between them.

2
The Classical View

It is only *au pays de la métaphore qu'on est poète*
(Wallace Stevens)

The Greeks were in no doubt that language was one of man's most distinctive features. It could even be used to define him. He was *zoon logon echon*, a living creature possessing speech, and it was this faculty as much as the faculty of reason (the same word *logos* signified both of them) which distinguished him from the other animals.

ARISTOTLE

Aristotle must then have been aware of the radical nature of what he was proposing when he made his careful disposition of the arts of language into three distinct categories; *logic, rhetoric* and *poetic*: categories which, his philosophy implies, could be considered as separate entities on the grounds that, as Richard McKeon puts it, 'different purposes and different criteria select different aspects of language to constitute different wholes from different parts.' In effect, this meant that the language of poetry would be distinct from the language of logic and rhetoric, and would have a different purpose in view.

The difference is largely a matter of metaphor. Poetry draws heavily on metaphor because of its involvement with the process of 'imitation', and its characteristic pursuit of 'distinctiveness' of expression. Logic and rhetoric, on the other hand, have 'clarity' and 'persuasion' as their respective goals and although they may use metaphor from time to time for certain effects, they are much more closely involved with the medium of prose and the structures of 'ordinary' speech.

It is clear enough, then, that in Aristotle's thinking the difference between the 'ordinary' or 'prose' use of words and the 'distinctive' or 'poetic' use of them is inherent. And in fact the notion of metaphor as a *departure* from the ordinary modes of language runs through all his writings on the subject.

It is in the *Poetics* (Chapters 21–25) and the *Rhetoric* (Book III) that Aristotle goes into the greatest detail on the subject of metaphor. He distinguishes four kinds within the general definition that 'Metaphor is the application to one thing of a name belonging to another thing'. The analysis is carried out in terms of content, not form, and the 'transference' involved may be as follows:

1. from the genus to the species ('Here *lies* my ship': 'lying' is a genus, 'lying at anchor' a species).
2. from the species to the genus ('*Ten thousand* good deeds': a specific number, used instead of the genus 'many').
3. from one species to another ('*Draining off* the life with the bronze', 'draining off' used in place of 'severing'. Both are species of 'taking away').
4. a matter of analogy.

(*Poetics*, Chap. 21)

Clearly, types 1 to 3 are closely related to each other in a way that 4 is not, and Aristotle devotes some time to an account of this last 'proportional' sort of metaphor, which he recognizes as the 'most taking' kind. If the first three types can be said to be 'simple' metaphors, type 4 could be termed complex, since it involves the use of analogy: 'I explain metaphor by analogy as what may happen when of four things the second stands in the same relationship to the first as the fourth to the third.' That is, the four elements of the metaphor, A, B, C, D, are connected in the way that B's relationship with A is analogous to D's relationship with C.

Thus, Aristotle says, a goblet stands in the same relationship to

Dionysus as a shield does to Ares. So, a goblet may be called 'the shield of Dionysus', and a shield may be called 'the goblet of Ares'. Old age is to life as evening is to day. So, one may call the evening the 'old age of the day'. When Pericles said that the death of the young men in the war was 'as if the spring were taken out of the year' he was using the 'proportional' type of metaphor. Indeed, liveliness can best be achieved by using this type of metaphor, 'and by being graphic' (i.e. by making your hearers *see* things) as well as by using metaphors 'that represent things as in a state of activity'. Thus 'with his vigour *in full bloom*'; 'the bitter arrow *flew*'; 'the point of the spear *in its fury* drove full through his breastbone'.

The simile is also considered as a kind of metaphor; 'the difference is but slight' (*Rhetoric* III, 1406b), and those which are successful 'always involve two relations like the proportional metaphor'. Indeed, 'a simile succeeds best when it is a converted metaphor': e.g. 'a ruin is like a house in rags'; those legs of his curl just like parsley leaves'. Proverbs are metaphors of type 3, and successful hyperboles are also metaphors rather in the manner of the simile, e.g., of a man with a black eye 'You would have thought he was a basket of mulberries' (it is implied that his eye was 'just like' a basket of mulberries).

Whatever else may be said of this analysis, it is abundantly clear that, as an entity in itself, metaphor is regarded as a decorative additive to language, to be used in specific ways, and at specific times and places. It will also be noticed that 'clarity' is presumed to reside in 'ordinary' language, which is non-metaphorical: metaphor is a kind of dignifying, enlivening ingredient, a set of 'unfamiliar usages' which, 'by the very fact of not being normal idiom' can '. . . raise the diction above the level of the commonplace'. The poet's medium includes the 'admixture of unfamiliar terms and metaphors and the various other modifications of language that are allowed to poets'. And we should remember that 'there are not the same standards of correctness in poetry as in political theory or any other art'. Metaphor is a kind of 'added extra' to language, the 'seasoning of the meat' (*Rhetoric* III, 1406a). Too much metaphor, we are warned, can make 'ordinary' language 'too much like poetry' (*Rhetoric* III, 1406b). And that, it is made plain, would never do.

The effect of metaphor 'properly' used is that by combining the familiar with the unfamiliar, it adds charm, and distinction, to clarity. Clarity comes from familiar 'everyday words', the 'proper or regular' class of terms used by everybody in conversation. Charm comes from the intellectual pleasure afforded by the new resemblances noted in the metaphor, distinction from the surprising nature of some of the resemblances discerned. The 'proper' use of metaphor also involves the principle of decorum. Metaphors must be 'fitting', i.e. in keeping with the theme or purpose. They must not be far-fetched or strange, and should make use of words which are beautiful in themselves.

Behind this view of metaphor there may be discerned two fundamental ideas about language and its relationship to the 'real' world; first, that language and reality, words and the objective world to which they refer, are quite separate entities; and second, that the *manner* in which something is said does not significantly condition or alter *what* is said. Those who think otherwise exhibit a defect:

> . . . we ought in fairness to fight our case with no help beyond the bare facts . . . Still . . . other things affect the result considerably, owing to the defects of our hearers . . . Not, however, (with) so much importance as people think. All such arts are fanciful and meant to charm the hearer. Nobody uses fine language when teaching geometry.
> (*Rhetoric* III, 1404a)

That is to say, there are 'bare facts', and there are various ways of talking about them which are separable from them. The 'real world' remains the same, however we speak of it. Language is a means of *describing* reality, but it cannot *change* it. Thus, the foundation of a good style is 'correctness of language', its aim is clarity, and its principal care is the avoidance of ambiguity,

> ... unless, indeed, you definitely desire to be ambiguous, as those do who have nothing to say but are pretending to mean something. Such people are apt to put that sort of thing into verse.
>
> (*Rhetoric* III, 1407a)

As well as leading to ambiguity, poetical effects are seen, outside poetry, almost as a vice of language, and certainly not as part of its 'normal' nature.

So, language's primary aim is to be transparent; to make manifest the 'bare facts' of reality. Certain distracting 'effects' possible in language are to be reserved for the realm of 'poetry' alone, or are only to be admitted elsewhere under strict supervision. And yet it is notable that the creative, educative aspect of metaphor is nevertheless clearly recognized by Aristotle. The use of metaphor is 'by far the most important thing to master'.

> This is one thing that cannot be learned from anyone else, and it is the mark of great natural ability, for the ability to use metaphor well implies a perception of resemblances.
>
> (*Poetics*, Chap. 22)

It enables us to 'get hold of new ideas';

> ... strange words simply puzzle us; ordinary words convey only what we know already; it is from metaphor that we can best get hold of something fresh.
>
> (*Rhetoric* III, 1410b)

In fact, metaphor is part of the learning process. The hearer is impressed by the liveliness of the metaphor, and the new idea it contains. Thus, the idea of old age as a 'withered stalk' conveys the new idea of lost bloom. A metaphor can have the novelty of a joke – 'his feet were shod with his chilblains' – and yet at the same time the hearer's mind encounters a new idea; it seems to say 'Yes, to be sure; I never thought of that.' Nevertheless, and oddly perhaps to a modern mind, Aristotle seems unable to extend this view of the capacities of metaphor into his concept of the nature of language at large. He does not even seem to grasp that the phrase 'the bare facts' is itself metaphorical.

CICERO, HORACE, LONGINUS

Where Aristotle had 'isolated' metaphor in his account of the four kinds, and had thus affirmed the notion of metaphor as some sort of special 'effect' that could be achieved in language employed in a 'special' way, subsequent classical writings on the subject seem largely to reinforce this tendency, to refine the results of this sort of analysis, and to stress more and more a principle of *decorum* in the matter, which insists on a necessary harmony or congruity between the elements of the metaphor. The traditional condemnation of 'mixed metaphor' is a natural consequence of such a principle.

Thus Cicero, for whom decorum was as J. W. H. Atkins says '... a principle of life transferred to the sphere of art', inevitably saw metaphor as one of the means of giving decorous 'effect' to speech. In it, '... you take what you have not got from somewhere else'. It is 'a sort of borrowing'.

> A metaphor is a short form of simile, contracted into one word; this word is put in a position not belonging to it as if it were its own place, and if it is recognizable it gives pleasure, but if it contains no similarity it is rejected.
>
> (*De Oratore* III, xxxviii, 155 ff.)

The metaphor should 'avoid all unseemliness' as well as obscurity and, in its decorous form, is one of a group of 'figures' whose role is cosmetic with respect to 'ordinary' language; '... a most effective way of introducing spots of high light to give brilliance to the style.'

Horace, in the *Art of Poetry*, whilst giving priority to usage (or convention) over abstract 'law' in the matter of language, nevertheless also advocates decorum in all things. Each style should be kept 'for the role properly allotted to it' and the metaphors used ought clearly to follow suit. Metaphor's role is to present relationships that are harmonious and 'true to life' rather than exploratory or novel.

Longinus in his *On The Sublime* lists the 'proper' formulation of figures of thought and figures of speech among the five sources of the grand style, and 'command of language' as that 'common foundation' without which 'sublimity' would be unachievable. However, it becomes clear that the rhetorical 'figures' remain, predictably, separable from 'ordinary' language, since they can readily be added to it as a '. . . means of increasing the animation and the emotional impact of style'. In particular, metaphors should only be used on 'appropriate' occasions, and not more than two 'or at most three' should be brought together in the same passage. The notion that metaphors 'contribute' to sublimity is of course part of the fundamental notion that the use of metaphor can and should be precisely controlled.

QUINTILIAN

Possibly the culmination of this sort of approach to language and to metaphor is to be found in Quintilian's *Institutio Oratoria*, which elegantly sums up most of what went before; it is, in Atkins' words, a 'restatement of classicism'. For Quintilian, art is an aspect of nature, and it reveals nature. Hence, although correctness in language is based on 'ordinary' speech, it is not limited to it, because ordinary speech is inadequate in itself, and needs to be raised to a higher power for the purposes of art. 'Figures of speech' and 'tropes' of course have just this 'raising' effect when used in a decorous manner. A trope consists of 'the artistic alteration of a word or phrase from its proper meaning to another', and 'the commonest and by far the most beautiful of tropes' is of course '*Metaphor*, the Greek term for our *translatio*'. Quintilian then distinguishes four kinds of metaphorical 'transference' or 'translation' somewhat in the manner of Aristotle, but along slightly different lines:

(i)   from the inanimate to the animate (the enemy is called a 'sword')
(ii) from the animate to the inanimate (the 'brow' of a hill)
(iii) from the inanimate to the inanimate ('He gave his fleet the rein')
(iv) from the animate to the animate ('Scipio was barked at by Cato')

Metaphor's ultimate value, it transpires, and one which obviously justifies its use of words and phrases in ways that are not 'proper', is that it is decorative. It is 'the supreme *ornament* of style'.

THE RHETORICA AD HERENNIUM

Quintilian is rightly considered representative of the ideas about metaphor that had been accumulated by the rhetoricians that preceded him, and his considerable influence on theorists and artists in the Renaissance makes his account of great interest. However, possibly the most exhaustive of such accounts, and one no less influential subsequently, is that given much earlier in the anonymous *Rhetorica ad Herennium* (c. 86 B.C.) – at one time falsely attributed to Cicero.

Characteristically perhaps, its emphasis in respect of metaphor is on decorum. The 'unusual' or 'mixed' metaphor is to be deplored:

Metaphor occurs when a word applying to one thing is transferred to another, because the similarity seems to justify the transference . . . They say that a metaphor ought to be restrained so as to be a transition with good reason to a kindred thing, and not seem an indiscriminate, reckless, and precipitate leap to an unlike thing.

– and six somewhat forbidding 'uses' of metaphor are recommended:

(a) for vividness
(b) for brevity
(c) to avoid obscenity
(d) for magnifying
(e) for minifying
(f) for embellishing

Book IV of the *Rhetorica ad Herennium* proceeds to an elaborate analysis of Figures of Diction and Figures of Thought which confer 'distinction' on style, and in this it represents perhaps the ultimate refinement of the sort of analysis begun by Aristotle. It lists 45 Figures of Diction, including 10 Tropes, of which Metaphor is one, and 19 Figures of Thought, of which Simile is one. Since sections of the *Rhetorica ad Herennium* found their way, as pure Ciceronian doctrine, into such English works as Wilson's *Arte of Rhetoric* (1553), its influence is of the same order of importance as Quintilian's *Institutio Oratoria* – which of course was itself influenced by it.

However, the simple 'trope of transference', metaphor, peeps out at us here with what seems – despite protestations to the contrary – considerably diminished stature. Where Aristotle had simply isolated metaphor, and distinguished four types of it, the *Rhetorica ad Herennium* and the later works of Cicero, Quintilian, and others, seem to *reduce* metaphor to one of a group of tropes which themselves form part of the merely decorative category of Figures of Speech. As such, it has no real claim to positive 'meaning' in its own right, since it works negatively by subverting the 'proper' meanings of words. So, although metaphor is usually said to be pre-eminent amongst the tropes, there can be little doubt that its isolation, first as a principle of 'poetic' language distinct from 'ordinary' language, and subsequently as one of the slightly suspect devices available to the stylist only for special ornamental 'effects', means that, in theory, it would be possible and in some circumstances perhaps desirable to have a language devoid of metaphor altogether.

3
Sixteenth, Seventeenth and Eighteenth Century Views

> Metaphor creates a new reality from which the
> original appears to be unreal
>
> (Wallace Stevens)

THE MIDDLE AGES

The Middle Ages were not notable for the development of literary theory, but they showed an interest in the process of formalizing and prescription that derived from the classical approach to metaphor, though it had a different end in view. The *Rhetorica ad Herennium* was a major model, and preceded the influence of Quintilian and Cicero which became very marked in the Renaissance.

A good example of medieval thinking is the Anglo-Norman Geoffrey of Vinsauf's *Poetria Nova*, which contains a complicated account of sixty-three poetical 'ornaments' divided into the categories of 'difficult' and 'easy', with close definitions of each one, and careful prescription of the situations and manner in which each should be used. In the matter of metaphor, Geoffrey somewhat arbitrarily reduces the animate-inanimate relationship stressed by Quintilian to one of human-non-human. He prefers, he says, metaphors in which the transference is from man to thing: flowers 'are born', the earth 'grows young', a process which we would simply term 'personification'. The whole thing perhaps seems pointlessly fussy to us.

However, it is important to understand the role given to metaphor in a society that is almost wholly Christian, and a failure to do so has led to serious misconceptions in our own time. We tend, after all, to think of metaphor as a means of achieving a direct linguistic realization of *personal* experience. Even banalities such as 'like a sledgehammer'; 'a hot knife through butter'; 'a bull in a china shop'; aim at a 'vivid' 'striking' and 'physical' quality that relates *accurately* to events in the world, and communicates something about them with some degree of exactitude. But in a Christian society, particularly of the pre-Reformation sort, the purely personal experience tends to be of less interest and importance than the experience of the society at large, manifested in its general view of the world it inhabits. Such a society's view of metaphor – and, indeed, its metaphors themselves – will naturally tend to relate to *collective* experience, and will concern themselves less with *personal accuracy* than with *public acceptability*.

For a Christian society, in the Middle Ages, a fundamental metaphor was that the world was a book written by God. And like any other book, it could and did 'mean' more than it apparently 'said'.

In fact, the world was full of metaphors, constructed by God to communicate a meaning when 'interpreted' properly. Words signified things, but things themselves had significance at another, higher level. The best exposition of the way in which metaphors should be interpreted in the light of this situation is given by Dante in his famous Letter to Can Grande della Scala, which prefaces the *Paradiso*, and concerns 'levels' of meaning in the whole *Commedia*. These are, first a *literal* meaning (the 'story' of the poem) and then three higher levels of meaning, the *allegorical* (the symbolic meanings appropriate to this world), the *anagogical* (those appropriate to the spiritual world), and the *tropological* (those appropriate to a personal or moral level).

These 'levels' of meaning require a function of metaphor which has very little to do with its capacity to give a truthful report of individual physical experience. Indeed individual physical experience would act as a red herring in a situation where the object of the poet was to deepen and extend the poem's meaning in relation to a theological framework. Equally, mere personal decoration would be a luxury, given such an aim. Far from expressing his *own* view of the world, and decorating it to suit his *own* delight, the poet's task is ultimately one of discovering *God's* meaning, and his metaphors are means to that end.

In a Christian world, then, classical rhetoricians were acceptable, but not as authorities in their own right, so much as emissaries of a higher authority. As Perry Miller puts it, by the end of the sixteenth century

> ... it was agreed on all sides that rhetoric was derived from God, that Aristotle and Quintilian, like the great prophets of Judea, had been essentially 'scribes' merely setting down a revelation from on high.
> (*The New England Mind*, p. 312)

DONNE AND THE COMPASSES

In her influential study, *Elizabethan and Metaphysical Imagery*, Rosamund Tuve takes great pains to establish a function for metaphor in the Elizabethan period of English literature that derives from these medieval principles, and which in essence involves the poet's refusal (in our terms) 'to narrow the task of images to that of a truthful report of experience'.

The Elizabethan poet, she argues, is not concerned to communicate real sensuous experience (i.e. 'this is how it felt to me') but to emphasize and reinforce what was felt to be an overall order beneath the surface differences of nature and the world. He is concerned with values and meanings that are not private and personal, but generally accepted and believed (i.e. 'this is how the world is arranged, isn't it?').

A modern poet constructs metaphors that realize, or attempt to

realize, personal responses to the world, and tries to convey these
with some degree of accuracy:

> They are rattling breakfast plates in basement kitchens,
> And along the trampled edges of the street
> I am aware of the damp souls of housemaids
> Sprouting despondently at area gates.
>
> (T. S. Eliot, *Morning at the Window*, 1917)

Here the transference of the qualities of some sort of dilapidated
and deprived plant growth to the housemaids' souls represents an
attempt to depict vividly and accurately their social and spiritual
state. The transference depends entirely on a highly personal set of
connections just barely visible to the reader. Indeed the tenuous-
ness of the connection contributes greatly to its effectiveness: like
the housemaid's soul, and the flower growing in the city street,
it is only just 'there'.

The seventeenth century poet, on the other hand, constructs his
metaphor from 'public' elements with 'established' ranges of
relationships. In general, his metaphors are self-consciously 'artificial' rather than sensuously vivid, designed to please on grounds
of formal excellence rather than by means of any 'likeness to the
stuff of life':

> There is a garden in her face,
> Where roses and white lilies grow;
> A heav'nly paradise is that place,
> Wherein all pleasant fruits do flow.
> There cherries grow, which none may buy
> Till 'Cherry-ripe' themselves do cry.
>
> (Thomas Campion, from *The Third and Fourth Booke of Ayres*, 1617)

Here the plants and the garden are selected as elements in the metaphor on grounds of their *appropriateness* rather than their *accuracy*.
They are appropriate, not because the lady's face in any way
physically resembles a garden, but because they enable the poet to

associate her beauty with the Garden of Eden, and her virginity with the innocence that pertained there. The lady thus takes her place in an ordered and unified world which links her virginity with a state of holy innocence embracing both the Virgin Mary and, until her death, England's Virgin Queen.

In short, metaphor in Elizabethan poetry represents an act of 'ordering' imposed on Nature. Its main principles are those of *decorum* or 'aptness', *consistency* and *coherence*. Its mode is artificial, because its aim is to be natural, and for the Elizabethan poet to be natural meant the *reverse* of being artless. The poet is like the gardener whose art 'helps' nature. In the words of George Puttenham, he 'furthers her conclusions and many times makes her effects more absolute and strange' (*The Arte of English Poesiee*, 1589). In a sense, the metaphor had a didactic role and was concerned to manifest truths, ideas and values that carried public assent. Its function was to reinforce an established view of the world, certainly not to challenge or question that view by means of a particular 'local' or 'singular' insight. Mere individual precision and accuracy of sensuous description would have seemed to have little point. The poet's metaphor draws attention, not to his own powers, but to God's who wrote the 'book' he is interpreting. The relationships that the metaphor establishes are created in the first place by God; the poet merely discovers them.

A good example is Donne's famous metaphor of the two lovers' souls and the compasses:

> If they be two, they are two so
> As stiffe twin compasses are two,
> Thy soule the fixt foot, makes no show
> To move, but doth, if th'other doe.
>
> And though it in the center sit,
> Yet when the other far doth rome,
> It leanes, and hearkens after it,
> And grows erect, as that comes home.

Such wilt thou be to mee, who must
Like th'other foot, obliquely runne;
Thy firmnes makes my circle just,
And makes me end, where I begunne.

(*A Valediction: forbidding mourning*)

There is nothing ironic here. As Miss Tuve says, 'It is to *us* rather than to Donne that compasses are part of the commonplace paraphernalia of high-school mathematics.' In the terms in which Donne was working, this metaphor exhibits decorum: it is uniquely suited to its subject, precisely apt for the purpose, and in no way shocking. It isn't even original. The compasses, which drew perfect circles, were acceptable symbols of perfection – as their circles were symbols of unity. The metaphor thus is consistent with the theme of the poem, and exemplifies the coherence of a world in which lovers and compasses have this relationship.

The result, aimed at and achieved here, is clarity. It is not the clarity of plainness (it is our modern prejudice that clarity cannot arise from profusion), for the aim is not to reproduce the mere visible world. As Miss Tuve puts it, the object of a metaphor of this sort is to reproduce the *intelligible* world; that is, the world that our intellects impose upon Nature, in accordance with our beliefs and our whole way of life. Given that, in a Christian society, the Deity is the focus of this way of life, Donne might well have regarded his metaphor as an instance of God's cleverness rather than his own. As a poet, he has, as it were, *discovered* the potential 'transference' between lovers and compasses, not *devised* it.

Quite clearly, Donne is experiencing a world fundamentally different from the one we inhabit, although modern critics have mistakenly taken his metaphors as if they were products of our own sort of culture. Yet it is clear that they spring from the heart of quite a different way of life. As Miss Tuve points out, there is nothing *extrinsic* about Donne's metaphors; they are not 'added' as a kind of *appliqué* work to his poetry.

Nor do they aim, to paraphrase the modern poet and theorist T. E. Hulme, at handing over sensations 'bodily' in order to make the reader 'continuously see a physical thing' (*Speculations* p. 134). While the Elizabethan poet was quite capable of constructing metaphors that would 'hand over' sensations directly from writer to reader, this was far from his main purpose. On the contrary, the Elizabethan metaphor's prime concern seems to have been to involve its audience in an *abstract* process, and to make it participate therein. In other words, it requires an audience to 'complete' it.

A metaphor's function, then, was *dramatic* (appropriately enough for a culture that was still predominantly oral in character), and in much of the best verse of the period a 'speaking' voice is heard, even in that verse which was not primarily designed for the age's greatest poetic vehicle, the drama.

In short, Elizabethan metaphors speak, and they ask for a response. Modern metaphors, by contrast, try to deliver their goods in one immediate 'handing over' which is complete in itself (appropriately enough for verse designed to be read in silence).

RAMUS

One of the most formative although indirect influences on the nature of metaphor at this time was probably the philosopher and rhetorician Peter Ramus (1515–72). Ramus' books were widely read and distributed throughout Europe, and his 'method' very quickly became a matter of virtually unquestioned orthodoxy.

Briefly, Ramus took the elaborate structure of traditional Aristotelian rhetoric, and methodically imposed upon it a division whose implications remain with us to this day. Traditionally, rhetoric had five parts; Invention, Disposition, Elocution, Memory and Delivery, and each part made an indispensable contribution to the construction of a good speech. Ramus simply split these into two groups, shifting Invention, Disposition and Mem-

ory under the heading of Dialectic (i.e. logic), and leaving
Rhetoric with only the remaining Elocution and Delivery.

Miss Tuve argues that the effect of Ramus on metaphor was in
general beneficial as far as Elizabethan and Metaphysical poetry
goes. Metaphor became, in a sense, more logical as poets made
more conscious attempts to relate Invention in poetry to logic.
Metaphors could be fruitfully constructed on a logical base, itself
deriving from the logical bases upon which all comparisons must
rest. It is by this sort of logic that the 'transferences' of the following passage are generated:

> Like untuned golden strings all women are,
> Which long time lie untouched will harshly jar.
> Vessels of brass oft handled brightly shine;
> What difference betwixt the richest mine
> And basest mould but use? . . .
>
> (Marlowe, *Hero and Leander* I, 229–33)

As Miss Tuve says, the formal nature of these metaphors is what
distinguishes them, and not any 'handing over' of sensation
whereby we are made to 'see a physical thing'. In her own words

> . . . realization of sensuous qualities is not pertinent to the effect of the
> figures; no situation is clearly visualized; a woman is a musical string,
> a brass vessel, rich mine, base mould, in quick succession, and she is all
> of them with reference to but one characteristic which all share – of no
> worth if unused.
>
> (*op. cit.*, p. 255)

That is, the logical base for all the metaphors in the passage is the
same: things are found to be alike on the basis of certain common
'places' of logic – here, common 'manner of suffering' or action
received, resulting in common effect, so that if A and B are
treated in the same way, the result C is common to both. Ramism
meant that, in short, poetry could be thought to be grounded in

logic, like all reasonable discourse, and therefore concerned with the arrangement of thought in an orderly manner. There was thus no need to keep poetry and logic in separate compartments. There is no difference between metaphors which concern 'feeling', and conceptual statements which concern 'thinking'. Metaphors *are* arguments to the Ramist, and since the laws of logic were the laws of thought, the poet must know and use *these* in constructing his metaphors, and not the laws of 'free association' made much of in modern composition. As a result, the so-called 'metaphysical' poem is able to dispense with mere rhetorical persuasion and to substitute for it intellectual probing. To quote Miss Tuve again,

> Functioning as units in a 'dialectical' discourse, images would have a logical toughness and an intellectual fineness which could stand to the tests of such discourse. Images would be many . . . for their usefulness and dignity as 'arguments' were unquestioned, and they could reach outward by the use of trope to further and deeper arguments . . . their chief characteristics would be aptness, subtlety, accuracy of aim, disregard of the superficially pleasing, logical power, ingenious or startlingly precise relationships or parallels, a certain 'obscurity' due to logical complexity or tenuous attachment – but an obscurity capable of becoming sharp 'clarity' upon thoughtful reading.
> These are normally the characteristics of Metaphysical imagery.
> (*op. cit.*, p. 353)

DRYDEN AND THE PIMPLES

In 1649, at the age of eighteen, Dryden composed some lines on the death from smallpox of Lord Hastings;

> Was there no milder way but the Small Pox,
> The very Filth'ness of *Pandora*'s Box?
> So many Spots, like *naeves*, our *Venus* soil?
> One Jewel set off with so many a Foil?
> Blisters with pride swell'd; which th'row 's flesh did sprout
> Like Rose-buds, stuck i' th' Lily-skin about.
> Each little Pimple had a Tear in it,

To wail the fault its rising did commit:
Who, Rebel-like, with their own Lord at strife,
Thus made an Insurrection 'gainst his Life.
Or were these Gems sent to adorn his Skin,
The Cab'net of a richer Soul within?

(ll. 53-64)

Terms such as 'aptness, subtlety, accuracy of aim' do not imme-
diately occur in connection with these metaphors, and although the
poet's meaning is clearly discernible, something has gone radically
wrong with its realization. The metaphors have little organic
relationship with their subject; they merely decorate it, like so
many ponderous afterthoughts, and succeed only in being ridicu-
lous. What went wrong?

The answer perhaps lies in a view of the effect of Ramus's
thinking on metaphor which is the opposite of that advanced by
Rosamund Tuve. Ramus's division of traditional Rhetoric had
certainly had its effect on Dialectic, and so on poetic Invention as
newly part of Dialectic, but it had had no less an effect upon
Rhetoric itself. Where Rhetoric had formerly embraced the
totality of the verbal arts, the requirements for hard, logical
thought together with those for beautifying ornament, Ramus's
division, reducing it to mere Elocution and Delivery, made it
merely a cosmetic repertoire of 'figures' or trimmings that could
be added to discourse after the logical arguments had been established. Rhetoric after Ramus becomes, in the words of Perry
Miller, the 'sugar on the pill of logic'. The sort of 'eloquence'
resulting from the new role given to Elocution is one which, as a
contemporary handbook put it, teaches us to express material '...
by apt wordes and sentences together, and beautifieth the tongue
with great chaunge of colours, and varietie of figures' (Perry
Miller, *The New England Mind*, p. 315).

Fundamentally, the Ramist division separates the content from
the form, the 'logic' of an argument from the stylistic embellish-

ment that may be applied to it to make it persuasive. By the same token, it makes of metaphor a merely pleasing device, serving only to prettify the 'message' of an utterance, and certainly not designed to make any contribution to it; it becomes a kind of fancy dress in which thoughts may from time to time be clothed; flowers culled from the garden of rhetoric with which a discourse might be decorated.

This, it could be argued, is what is wrong with Dryden's metaphor of the pimples. Unlike Donne's metaphor of the compasses, it lacks an innate connection between its elements, the argument, and the total society from which that argument derives, and to which it is relevant. Dryden's metaphors in those lines are 'applied' to the argument from the outside, they do not arise organically from the inside. And although, conceived in the abstract, they might seem appropriate (their theme is the political one of rebellion seen as disease, and vice versa), when realized they become ludicrous and sensationally distasteful.

Ramists and others, particularly Puritans, were well aware of the absurd excesses to which this notion of Rhetoric's function could give rise. In fact the Ramist method of formal 'explanation' of an argument laid great emphasis on qualities of 'clarity' and 'distinctness' of a sort that metaphor could only seem to disrupt. Walter J. Ong has pointed out that in consequence the written text rather than the spoken utterance was favoured; the visual abstraction of writing being preferred to the oral reality of speech. By comparison with the written word, the non-visual word began to appear ephemeral and fugitive. And as a result the new renaissance technology of print was gradually invested with a sense of permanence denied to the living language; the maxim *verba volant, scripta manent*, seemed irrefutable. As Ong expresses it,

> ... at the heart of the Ramist enterprise is the drive to tie down words themselves, rather than other representations, in simple geometrical

patterns. Words are believed to be recalcitrant insofar as they derive from a world of sound, voices, cries; the Ramist ambition is to neutralize this connection by processing what is of itself nonspatial in order to reduce it to space in the starkest way possible.

(*Ramus, Method, and the Decay of Dialogue*, p. 89)

Where communication in the pre-Ramist world was

richly sonorous rather than merely 'clear' for it was the echo of a cognitive world experienced as if filled with sound and voices and speaking persons . . .

(p. 212)

the Ramist 'pedagogical juggernaut' eliminated sound and voice from man's understanding of the intellectual world, and created a situation in which 'Speech is no longer a medium in which the human mind and sensibility lives. It is resented . . .' (p. 291). As a result,

By its very structure, Ramist rhetoric asserts to all who are able to sense its implications that there is no way to discovery or to under- standing through voice, and ultimately seems to deny that the pro- cesses of person-to-person communication play any necessary role in intellectual life.

(p. 288)

It is a situation which the modern world has inherited, in the form of a rarely questioned dichotomy between speech and writing which invests the latter with an authority in matters of 'correct- ness', 'grammar' and ultimately 'logic', that it systematically denies to the former.

PLAIN STYLE

Given this division, and the role implicit in it for metaphor, it is hardly surprising that the Puritan mind, anxious to rid itself of the merely decorative in all spheres, should conceive the notion of a literary 'style' which made little or no use of metaphor at all. The modern diminution of Rhetoric, and its adjective, 'rhetorical', to the sense of the merely verbose and 'flowery' comes directly from this idea. Ong describes the seventeenth century configuration of Ramus's division in terms of man's fundamental activity, speech:

> Rhetorical speech is speech which attracts attention to itself as speech – the showy, the unusual . . . Dialectical or logical speech is speech which attracts no attention to itself as speech, the normal, the plain, the undistinguished, the reporter of 'things' . . .
>
> (p. 129)

The style that emerged from this opposition – it was a Puritan style of preaching – was called Plain Style.

The ideal of Plain Style is perhaps best expressed by the theologian William Ames (1576–1633) who said that the efficacy of the Holy Spirit 'doth more cleerely appeare in a naked simplicity of words, than in elegance and neatnesse'. 'Plaine delivery' of the word was the aim, 'painted eloquence' the enemy. Content was more important than form. Metaphor, if it had to be used at all, could be added later.

A good example of the sort of role this imposed on metaphor can be seen from the following examples. This is from one of John Donne's sermons:

> Let the head be gold, and the armes silver, and the belly brasse, if the feete be clay, Men that may slip, and molder away, all is but an Image, all is but a dreame of an Image; for forraine helps are rather crutches then legs. There must be bodies, Men, and able bodies, able men; Men that eate the good things of the land, their owne figges and olives; Men not macerated with extortions: They are glorified bodies that make up the kingdome of Heaven; bodies that partake of the good of the State, that make up the State.

The metaphors seem to flow naturally out of the material, and are part of it. We seem to hear a speaking voice, whose resonance, timbre and tone are inseparable from what it says. Compare this, which is the Puritan John Cotton, distinguishing between a true saint and a hypocrite:

Observe when those ends part, which will be at one time or other. When two men walk together, a dog follows them, you know not whose it is, but let them part, then the dog will follow his Master.

The metaphor of the men and the dog here is *added* to the point that has previously been made. It 'illustrates' the point, but in a real sense is extraneous to it. It embellishes the argument, but it is not an essential *part* of it. It has a 'written-down' air.

In effect, the cleavage between form and content, metaphor and language was complete, and the tendencies we have noticed in the later classical rhetoricians are here triumphantly reinforced in seventeenth century England and America. To the Ramist rhetoricians, metaphor is some kind of unusual 'ornamentation' of language. There is no sense of metaphor's *semantic* function or possibilities and as a result, in the words of Ong, their rhetoric textbooks which attempt to describe metaphors, tropes and figures, turn out to be an 'attempt to describe and classify the unusual without being able to identify what the usual is'.

The notion of 'ornament' as the function of rhetoric at large and of metaphor in particular will obviously and ultimately have its effect on the notion of language. And as the written language expanded its dominance over the older oral culture of the seventeenth century, so the auditory and resonant aspects of language tended to be reduced to the level of the visually comprehensible. Richard Baxter's (1615–91) dictum that 'painted obscure' sermons were 'like the Painted Glass in the Windows that keep out the Light' exhibits this strongly visual cast of mind, and of metaphor. Most recommendations to 'plainness' carry this covert emphasis on 'perspicuity', on the necessity for clear visual apprehension of the object 'through' the language.

Hence, if Rhetoric becomes the art of expressing oneself ornately, it also becomes a kind of visual art. Speech gives pride of place to writing. Metaphors become colours in a palette, and their use a kind of *appliqué* work, removed from the sound of the human voice, and distinct from logic altogether. Tropes become physical not acoustic things, spatial and diagrammatic 'turnings' of language from the straight and narrow path of meaning. Figures become physical 'shapes' carefully placed along the way. When Thomas Sprat, in his *History of the Royal Society*, condemning all use of tropes and figures, expresses his fears for the members that 'the whole spirit and vigour of their Design had been soon eaten out, by the luxury and redundance of *speech*' we might reasonably sense the beginning of another age.

THE EIGHTEENTH CENTURY

The essence of the Ramist revolution was the reduction of the personalized resonant human world of sound to a depersonalized silent world of space. In terms of language, it meant a reduction from the richly ambiguous multi-level meanings of the voice engaged in dialogue, to the evenly-spaced single-level 'clarity' of the written word. In literary terms it involves a shift of emphasis from the oral mode of drama (and much of the best Elizabethan and Jacobean poetry is fundamentally 'dramatic' dialogue, even if as in Shakespeare's sonnets, it is one-sided), to the literate mode of the printed book. In terms of a larger outlook it might be said to mark the transition from an ancient world to a recognizably modern one.

The pursuit of 'clarity' and 'distinction' naturally took its toll of metaphor. If we return to Thomas Sprat we find a characteristically unequivocal statement in praise of the members of the Royal Society:

> They have therefore been most rigorous in putting in execution, the only Remedy, that can be found for this extravagance: and that has been, a constant Resolution, to reject all the amplifications, digressions, and swellings of style: to return back to the primitive purity, and shortness, when men delivered so many things, almost in an equal number of words. They have exacted from all their members, a

close, naked, natural way of speaking: positive expressions; clear senses; a native easiness: bringing all things as near the Mathematical plainness, as they can.

(History of the Royal Society, 1667)

The 'extravagance', say, of Dryden's metaphor of the pimples might be a welcome casualty of this sort of stringency, but the precise relationship between words and things here obviously hoped for could only reinforce the notion of metaphor as some kind of special added 'ornament' to a language which, if left metaphor-less, would carry its meanings simply, naturally, and more efficiently.

It was a persuasive outlook, and it carried the day. Indeed, in 1670, Samuel Parker went so far as to advocate an Act of Parliament forbidding the use of 'fulsome and luscious' metaphors. Ultimately, even so perspicacious a critic as Dr Johnson could take a somewhat jaundiced view of the metaphors of the previous century. His comment of the 'wit' of the metaphysicals is well-known:

the most heterogeneous ideas are yoked by violence together; nature and art are ransacked for illustrations, comparisons, and allusions; their learning instructs and their subtilty surprises; but the reader commonly thinks his improvement dearly bought and, though he sometimes admires, is seldom pleased.

(The Life of Cowley, 1779)

In fact it is precisely the notion that 'poetic' language is fundamentally different from 'ordinary' language and that the two should be kept firmly apart that generates his comment on Shakespeare's brilliant metaphor, uttered by Lady Macbeth,

> Come thick night
> And pall thee in the dunnest smoke of hell,
> That my keen knife see not the wound it makes,
> Nor heaven peep through the blanket of the dark,
> To cry 'Hold, hold!'

(I, v, 48–52)

Johnson is amused and dismayed by such 'low' words, arguing that

> the efficacy of this invocation is destroyed by the insertion of an epithet now seldom heard but in the stable, and *dun* night may come or go without any other notice than contempt. . . . (the) sentiment is weakened by the name of an instrument used by butchers and cooks in the meanest employments; we do not immediately conceive that any crime of importance is to be committed with a *knife* . . . while I endeavour to impress on my reader the energy of the sentiment, I can scarce check my risibility when the expression forces itself upon my mind; for who, without some relaxation of his gravity, can hear of the avengers of guilt *peeping through a blanket*?
>
> *(Rambler* No. 168, 1751)

In the definition given in Johnson's great *Dictionary* there is the sense, almost, of metaphor as an *abuse* of language. It is 'The application of a word to an use to which, in its original import, it cannot be put.' Language was the 'dress' of thought and metaphor was part of the mere mode of 'expression' which the writer chose to embellish the thought. In Pope's terms, then, true wit itself should manifest this division. It should be 'what oft was thought, but ne'er so well expressed'. Or, to use terms made current by the philosopher Hobbes, the faculty of Judgement exercised a controlling role in deciding what a poem was to be about, and then another faculty, Fancy, took on the task of decorating the poem with suitable metaphors. To quote Dr. Johnson again, 'As to metaphorical expression, that is a great excellence in style, when it is used with propriety, for it gives you two ideas for one.'

Hence the notion that metaphors could be *computed*; that verse could be *too* metaphorical. Pope rewrote Donne, in much the same spirit that Dryden, in *All for Love* had rewritten Shakespeare's *Antony and Cleopatra*, removing the ambiguities engendered by a language which, like all languages, was naturally metaphorical, and substituting for them a new 'clarity' so that the unencumbered 'thought' might unambiguously emerge. The new 'clarity' could hardly of course have a personal cast. If it was clear, it was so because it was 'general' and not personal. It was, in essence, a product of language when it is written down, and standardized. In such a process, ambiguity becomes a vice, and the arbiter of meaning is not the individual speaker who explains himself by tone of voice, gesture, physical presence, but the Dictionary. Eighteenth century metaphors tend to deal in what is generally and universally acceptable. They need no audience to 'complete' them, to respond to, or join in with any thought-process that springs from the centre of a culture. They are at their worst pre-packaged, pre-digested, finished products, unloaded strategically in the poem when triggered by taste. The result is a far cry from ordinary language, and indeed is far enough to sustain a belief that poetry should be written in a 'special' language of its own; a language anaesthetized to many of the resources of ordinary speech, and to which we have given the name Poetic Diction.

4
The Romantic View

> There is a nature that absorbs the mixedness of
> metaphors
>
> (Wallace Stevens)

According to John Stuart Mill, Coleridge used to say that every-
one is born either a Platonist or an Aristotelian. Notions of metaphor certainly seem to confirm and reinforce the same distinction,
and those poets and theorists who can be classed under the
Romantic faction tend to reject utterly the Aristotelian 'classical'
notion that metaphor is in some way 'detachable' from language;
that it is a kind of device that can be added to language the better
to fit it for a certain task or function.

Instead, in sharp reaction to the Aristotelian thinking of the pre-
ceding century, they tend to proclaim metaphor's 'organic' relationship to language as a whole, and to lay stress on its vital
function as an expression of the faculty of imagination. The three
main expositors of this view all claimed, at some time or other, to
be followers of Plato.

PLATO
Of course, being a 'follower of Plato' is rather like being a
'follower' of Marx or Freud, in that it does not presuppose (or
apparently necessitate) any knowledge of what the relevant
luminary actually said. In the case of Plato the position is perhaps
excusably complicated by the existence of a large body of what has
(often loosely) been termed 'neo-Platonic' writing, which was
available to and certainly read by the Romantic poets. There is,

however, often a significant difference between the Platonic and the neo-Platonic.

In fact, unlike Aristotle, Plato gives no overt general account either of language or of metaphor. However he does express some views of an apparently casual nature which may contain a clue as to why the Romantic poets felt drawn to the philosopher who, above all others, professed to be the enemy of poets.

In the dialogue called *Cratylus*, for example, the discussion centres on the origin of names. And the argument turns on whether language may be said to be fundamentally conventional and arbitrary in its relationship to the world, or whether there exists some sort of 'inherent correctness' in names: whether the determining factor in the ascription of words to things is ordinary usage, or whether there are natural 'laws' governing the process. What emerges from the argument is a surprising readiness to give *custom* and *convention* their due; an active and informing awareness that language is concretely governed by organic principles springing from within itself, as much as by any 'laws' conceived in abstraction and imposed from outside. And this awareness can seem to inform the views Plato expresses on the major *art* of language, poetry.

One of the principles of art most clearly enunciated by Plato is that of organic unity. Every discourse, he says in the *Phaedrus*, should be 'constructed like a living creature'. That is, it cannot profitably be divided into its constituent parts, any more than these, in conjunction, can simply constitute the whole. Similarly, language is a whole and, unlike Aristotle, Plato doesn't seem overtly to want to violate its unity: he doesn't separate *poetic* language from the language of *rhetoric*.

It may well be that the Romantics found in this the basis of and justification for his famous animus against poets. If language is governed by organic principles, it is misleading to abstract any so-called 'part' of it from the whole. And yet *this* is exactly what the poet covertly proposes to do. He proposes to abstract the 'poetic' – or what we might call the 'metaphorical' – part of language, and to claim that as his own. *His* self-conscious claim to that particular function robs us of *our* unconscious rights to it as native speakers. And yet the truth is, the poet has no special access to any particular kind of language or knowledge (this case is presented in the *Ion*) that is denied to other people.

In fact, the poet's art pre-empts just those aspects of language which, in an oral community, are vital to ordinary rewarding interaction. Rhythm, rhyme, metaphor, the necessary elements in the mnemonic structures by whose means an oral society transmits its own identity from generation to generation, are powerful agents in the preservation and reinforcement of its way of life. The absence of such powerful elements obviously deals the abstract reasoning of philosophy a severe blow. It is denied access to the most effective way of making complex contact with the non-literate mind. And the mnemonic effects of poetry make people difficult to 'reach' and change by other means.

Truth for Plato resides in the activities of the philosopher, the dialectician, whose language derives from that fundamental model of all human communication, ordinary oral dialogue. The existence of 'poets' presupposes the absence of the vitalizing metaphorical elements of language from ordinary oral dialogue. Indeed, the existence of 'poetry' as a language peculiar to poets brings, by definition, a dilapidated 'ordinary' language into being.

SHELLEY, HERDER, VICO

If this is not what Plato *actually* meant, it is perhaps what the Romantics wanted him to mean, particularly in connection with their ideas of language, metaphor, and the working of the imaginative faculty. It is important to understand that the Romantic notion of the Imagination establishes and stresses that faculty's *connective* power, and sets it against the *divisive* character of another faculty, sometimes termed the Reason, but which for convenience may be thought of as a faculty of discursive analysis. This faculty discerns the differences between things, and their different relations to each other. Aristotle's analysis of metaphor is a good example of it in action. On the other hand, the Imagination is an active force of tremendous power, sufficient, in Wordsworth's words, 'to produce such changes even in our physical nature as might almost appear miraculous' (*Preface to the Lyrical Ballads*). Its characteristic ability is supremely that of drawing things together, of establishing powerful and unifying inter-relationships, similarities, links. It perceives and creates unity, of the sort that concerned Plato.

Thus, for the Romantics, the difference between Plato and Aristotle could be thought of (with breathtaking oversimplification) as more or less the same as the difference between Imagination and Reason. As Shelley (a 'Platonist') puts it in his *Defence of Poetry* (written 1821, published 1840), 'Reason respects the differences and imagination the similitudes of things.' He adds that poetry 'may be defined to be "the expression of the imagination"'.

Here lies the Imagination's central connection with metaphor. Poetry nourishes, it 'enlarges the circumference' of the Imagination by means of new combinations of thoughts which form 'new intervals and interstices' in it. The process, which 'strengthens that faculty . . . in the same manner as exercise strengthens a limb', is one of metaphor. The act of unifying, of inculcated 'sameness' which is metaphor's stock-in-trade, both stimulates and manifests the Imagination.

It follows that Imagination will embody itself in man's distinctive feature of language in the form of metaphor. Shelley has no hesitation in asserting that 'poetry is connate with the origin of man' and that it '. . . springs from the nature itself of language' which in turn is 'produced by the imagination and has relation to thoughts alone.' He adds, in words that Plato would presumably have approved, that in the 'infancy of society' all authors are poets 'because language itself is poetry', and 'in the youth of the world' those who are 'poets in the most universal sense of the word' speak a language which

> . . . marks the before unapprehended relations of things and per-
> petuates their apprehension until the words which represent them
> become, through time, signs for portions or classes of thoughts
> instead of pictures of integral thoughts.

It is a language which he terms 'vitally metaphorical'.

Such 'primitivist' notions had found expression much earlier and elsewhere in Europe. The German critic J. G. Herder for example, in his essay on the origin of language, *Abhandlung über den Ursprung der Sprache* (1772) conceives of primitive man thinking in symbols, and connects metaphor with the beginning of speech itself. The earliest language was a 'dictionary of the soul' and in it metaphors and symbols combined to create 'mythology and a marvellous epic of the actions and speeches of all beings – a constant fable with passion and interest.' The 'modern' poet is thus also a 'primitive' man, and he does not merely 'present' meaning, or 'imitate' nature, he *creates* these, as the savage creates fable and myth.

Before this, although unnoticed by his contemporaries, the distinguished Italian jurist and rhetorician Giambattista Vico had published his *New Science* (1725) in which he had similarly conceived of primitive man possessed of an instinctive 'poetic' wisdom (*sapienza poetica*) which evolved through metaphors, symbols and myths towards modern abstract and analytical modes of thought. We live in a world of words, made for us by our language, where 'minds are formed by the character of language, not language by the minds of those who speak it.'

In such a world, the principle of *verum factum* pertains. The true (*verum*) and the made (*factum*) are the same. Society is entirely made by man, and contains in itself the only truth he can really hope to know. In order to obtain a proper historical perspective for this truth, and to avoid imposing on it our own quite relative standards, Vico proposed an examination of the way in which the kinds of language men used, and the myths and fables they invented, led to the societies in which they occurred. This strikingly modern approach is the first systematic exposition of what has been lately termed the principle of 'cultural relativity', whereby an attempt is made to understand a culture in its own terms, and not by reference to some abstract model of how men in general are thought to behave.

Vico was led by these interests naturally to the study of children. The movement from childhood to maturity is a version, he argued, of that from 'primitive' societies to 'civilized' ones. And the language of children is essentially robust, vigorous and concrete compared to the abstract distinctions and categories of adult 'rational' speech. So 'primitive' legends and myths were not *lies*, so much as poetic, *metaphorical* responses to the world on the part of wholly responsible people. The metaphors often fossilized in current speech were once the live embodiments of vivid perceptions of whose existence we are unaware in our anaesthetized 'rational' world. Indeed, the very distinction we make between the 'literal' and the 'metaphorical' is only available in societies which have acquired the capacity for abstract thought. It is unavailable where thought is 'concrete', as in the case of children, or in what the modern French anthropologist Claude Lévi-Strauss has termed the 'savage mind'.

Metaphor, in short, is not fanciful 'embroidery' of the facts. It is a way of *experiencing* the facts. It is a way of thinking and of living; an imaginative projection of the truth. As such, it is at the heart of the 'made'.

It is interesting now to follow these ideas further, in the writings of the two major English Romantic theorists who succeeded Vico, and preceded Shelley; Wordsworth and Coleridge.

WORDSWORTH

Wordsworth's commitment to the 'language really used by men' certainly suggests a feeling on his part that such language is 'vitally metaphorical' in itself, and his *Preface to the Lyrical Ballads* confirms this. His interest in 'low and rustic life' derives largely, he tells us, from the 'plainer and more emphatic language' which it manifests, itself a product of hourly communication with 'the best objects from which the best part of language is originally derived'. This results in 'simple and unelaborated expressions' and in poetry ideas which 'are expressed in language fitted to their respective importance'.

> . . . such a language arising out of repeated experience and regular feelings is a more permanent, and a far more philosophical language than that which is frequently substituted for it by Poets.

And whilst this Vico-esque concern

> . . . has necessarily cut me off from a large portion of phrases and figures of speech which from father to son have long been regarded as the common inheritance of Poets

– he is content to do without such 'poetic' diction in favour of metaphors *organically* related to and arising from 'the language really spoken by men'. The reader should not be 'utterly at the mercy of the Poet respecting what imagery or diction he may choose to connect with the passion' for

> if the Poet's subject be judiciously chosen, it will naturally, and upon fit occasion, lead him to passions the language of which, if selected truly and judiciously, must necessarily be dignified and variegated, and alive with metaphors and figures.

Wordsworth's point is easily substantiated by means of a comparison of the sort of metaphors considered to be the 'common inheritance of poets' at the time

> For thee the fields their flowery carpet spread
> And smiling Ocean smooths his wavy bed;
> A purer glow the kindling poles display,
> Robed in bright effluence of ethereal day,
> When through her portals bursts the gaudy spring,
> And genial Zephyr waves his balmy wing.
> First the gay songsters of the feather'd train
> Feel thy keen arrows thrill in every vein ...
>
> (from the *Monthly Magazine*, February 1797)

– with those he constructed himself for the volume of *Lyrical Ballads* (1799):

> She dwelt among th'untrodden ways
> Beside the springs of Dove,
> A maid whom there were none to praise,
> And very few to love.
>
> A violet by a mossy stone
> Half-hidden from the eye!
> Fair as a star, when only one
> Is shining in the sky.

Here the reader finds himself firmly 'in the company of flesh and blood', and he hears the voice of 'a man speaking to men', whose sensibility differs only in degree, not kind, from that of other men. Indeed, a poet's language is 'defective' if it seems to emanate from that 'body of men who, from the circumstance of their compositions being in metre, it is expected will employ a particular language.'

If there is no 'special' language for poets, there can be no 'special' linguistic devices 'reserved' for poetry. This is at the heart of Wordsworth's argument that there exists no essential difference between the language of prose and that of verse. Prose and verse 'both speak by and to the same organs . . . Poetry sheds no tears "such as Angels weep" but natural and human tears; she can boast of no celestial Ichor that distinguishes her vital juices from those of prose; the same human blood circulates through the veins of them both.' Only when this is accepted will the chief pleasure of poetry be achieved, the sense of a particular human process in action.

This process is obviously felt by Wordsworth to occupy a central place in human experience. It is part and parcel of his interest in tracing in his poems 'the primary laws of our nature' chiefly in regard to 'the manner in which we associate ideas in a state of excitement'. It is a process, as he described it in *The Prelude*, of

> . . . observation of affinities
> In objects where no brotherhood exists
> To passive minds.
>
> (*The Prelude*, 1850, II, 384–6)

It is a process which constitutes 'the great spring of the activity of our minds, and their chief feeder', and

> From this principle the direction of the sexual appetite and all the passions connected with it, take their origin: it is the life of our ordinary conversation; and upon the accuracy with which similitude in dissimilitude, and dissimilitude in similitude are perceived, depend our taste and moral feelings.

It is, of course, the 'linking', unifying process of metaphor.

COLERIDGE

Coleridge's interest in 'the perception of similitude in dissimilitude' and, more generally, the entire 'manner in which we associate ideas' is well known, and could be said to lie at the centre of his thinking about the human faculty of the Imagination.

By its very name, the Imagination is connected with the making of images, and its relationship to the concept of metaphor is a

THE ROMANTIC VIEW 43

radical one. The fundamental notion that emerges from Coleridge's thinking and practice as a poet and a critic is that the ultimate realization of the Imagination will take linguistic form, and that that form is most obviously manifested in the sort of association of ideas which generates metaphor. One of the first Englishmen to have read and pondered the work of Vico, Coleridge conceives of metaphor as Imagination in action.

His notion of the mind was genuinely revolutionary. He saw it as 'an active, self-forming, self-realizing system' (I. A. Richards, *Coleridge on Imagination*) which, far from being passive in the face of so-called 'reality', actually imposed itself on the world, and creatively adapted and shaped it. Imagination acts as the chief instrument in this process. Almost literally, Imagination 'makes up' the world as it goes along. The most obvious and ideal instance of the process in human beings is, of course, the poet:

> The poet, described in ideal perfection, brings the whole soul of man into activity, with the subordination of its faculties to each other according to their relative worth and dignity. He diffuses a tone and spirit of unity that blends, and (as it were) *fuses*, each into each, by that synthetic and magical power, to which I would exclusively appropriate the name of Imagination.
>
> (*Biographia Literaria* Chap. XIV)

The function of this faculty is to connect, to fuse, to blend and to reconcile in a process of unification for which Coleridge coined the term 'esemplastic', which he said meant 'to shape into one'. It is a process which, to use the account Shelley gave of 'vitally metaphorical' language, '. . . marks the before unapprehended relations of things and perpetuates their apprehension.' And of course, in poetry, the process is exactly discernible:

> This power, first put into action by the will and understanding, and retained under their irremissive, though gentle and unnoticed control, *laxis effertur habenis*, reveals itself in the balance or reconcilement of opposite or discordant qualities: of sameness, with difference; of the

general with the concrete; the idea with the image; the individual with the representative; the sense of novelty and freshness with old and familiar objects; a more than usual state of emotion with more than usual order; judgement ever awake and steady self-possession with enthusiasm and feeling profound or vehement; and while it blends and harmonizes the natural and the artificial, still subordinates art to nature; the manner to the matter; and our admiration of the poet to our sympathy with the poetry.

(ibid.)

In the terms we have been using, it is quite easy to see this process as coterminous with that of metaphor, and in elaborating his theory, Coleridge uses specific analysis of metaphors to pinpoint some rather abstract distinctions.

The fundamental principle of Coleridge's philosophy is organicism. Like a true Platonist, he wished to discover the *organic* connection of all things, and to destroy the artificial boundaries between them constructed by Aristotelian analysis. In this, he can be said to have inherited the distinction between Classical and Romantic art that came to him from Germany through the work of the Schlegels, Goethe and Schiller.

Classical art is concerned to point out the balanced harmony existing in a well-ordered nature. Its basic principle is one of decorum, whereby elements are fitted to their proper classes and types, which are carefully distinguished (the Aristotelian accounts of metaphor itself come to mind as examples of this process). The Romantic concern is the depiction of a unity that lies underneath surface distinctions, and which ignores clear-cut boundaries.

Thus, in 'classical' drama, 'fixed' types of character are manipulated in connection with certain universal and abstract aims and values. The classical play moves in accordance with preconceived 'rules' and patterns to demonstrate certain principles that exist, as it were 'outside' the play.

The Romantic dramatist, on the other hand, concerns himself with concrete issues, and with the 'inward nature' of the characters involved. His play obeys no 'rules' except those which spring from within itself, and manifest its own organic, concrete necessities. Chief amongst the Romantic dramatists for Coleridge was of course Shakespeare, and his essay on *The Tempest* is one of the best examples of this kind of thinking in action.

The Tempest, he says, is supremely 'a specimen of the romantic drama; i.e. of a drama, the interests of which are independent of all historical facts and associations, and arise from their fitness to that faculty of our nature, the imagination I mean, which owns no allegiance to time and place . . . It addresses itself entirely to the imaginative faculty.' (*Coleridge on Shakespeare* p. 224.) As a result, the play manifests 'organic regularity' and not its 'mechanic' opposite.

Part of its organic quality resides of course in its use of metaphor, and Coleridge's comments on Shakespeare's metaphors are very revealing. The previous century's difficulties in this connection are of course notorious, none more so perhaps than some of those of Dr Johnson. His comment on the metaphor in *Macbeth*

> Here lay Duncan
> His silver skin laced with his golden blood
>
> II, iii, 108–9

is justly famous:

> No amendment can be made to this line, of which every word is equally faulty, but by a general blot. It is not improbable that Shakespeare put these forced and unnatural metaphors into the mouth of Macbeth as a mark of artifice and dissimulation . . .
>
> (Notes on *The Plays of Shakespeare* 1765.)

What Johnson is looking for is a 'classical' kind of distinction between the elements of the metaphor; a precise visual picture or 'image' of the *abstract* qualities referred to. What confronts him is, by the standards of those 'Aristotelian' requirements, plainly absurd. How can skin be 'silver' or blood 'golden'?

In fact, in Coleridge's terms – and they are, by contrast,

'Platonic' – such a metaphor shows exactly the Imagination's 'esemplastic' power at work. The terms 'silver' and 'golden' refer to Duncan's royal status over and above the reference they make to his physical body, rather in the same way that that status exists beyond its physical embodiment in him. As elements in the metaphor they are 'fused' and blended into a *concrete* unity, despite their abstract nature and function, independently of the 'mechanic' requirements of 'historical facts and associations', and the allegiances of 'time and space'. The result is a highly complex meaning with more than one level, addressed entirely to the imaginative faculty rather than to the reason, and revealing in itself 'the balance or reconcilement of opposite or discordant qualities.'

So, in his essay on *The Tempest*, Coleridge argues strongly against the 'mechanic' sort of metaphor whose elements are precisely arranged in Aristotelian relationships one to another. He stresses that

> The power of poetry is, by a single word perhaps, to instil that energy into the mind which compels the imagination to produce the picture. Prospero tells Miranda,
>
> > One midnight,
> > Fated to the purpose, did Antonio open
> > The gates of Milan; and i' the dead of darkness,
> > The ministers for the purpose hurried thence
> > Me, and thy crying self.
>
> Here, by introducing a single happy epithet, 'crying', in the last line, a complete picture is presented to the mind, and in the production of such pictures the power of genius consists.
>
> (*Coleridge on Shakespeare* pp. 233–4)

Later on, he defends from 'the very severe but inconsiderate censure of Pope and Arbuthnot' Prospero's elaborate metaphor by which he directs Miranda's attention to Ferdinand,

> The fringed curtains of thine eye advance,
> And say what thou seest yond.
>
> (I, ii, 408–9)

on the grounds of its *organic* relation to the play, and to Prospero's development in it (Prospero has the role and air throughout of a magician-cum-dramatist; he is about to 'produce' Ferdinand before Miranda surprisingly, and the metaphor gives the sense of an imminent act of prestidigitation, of a curtain about to rise on a marvellous sight).

Coleridge is careful to distinguish two aspects of the imaginative process: that of the so-called Primary Imagination, which perceives and operates within the 'ordinary world', and that of the so-called Secondary Imagination which re-works this world, and impresses its own shape upon it. *Words* are the means to this end. And the process, whereby words construct a 'reality' from within themselves, and impose this on the world in which we live, is a process of metaphor.

Coleridge is careful to juxtapose another faculty to Imagination, and to assign it an inferior function. He terms it the Fancy. If Imagination is a unifying 'esemplastic' power, Fancy is merely a power of assembly or collocation, involving simply the mechanical noting of resemblances (in the manner, somewhat, of Hartley's 'association of ideas'). And the sort of distinction Coleridge draws between the kinds of metaphor produced by Fancy on the one hand and by Imagination on the other is extremely interesting.

Fancy is 'the faculty of bringing together images dissimilar in the main, by some one point or more of likeness distinguished'. Such images have no 'natural or moral' connection, but are constructed by the poet on the basis of 'some accidental coincidence'. That is, Fancy represents mere aggregation, mere noting of factitious 'similarities' between things. As an example of this, he points to these lines from Shakespeare's *Venus and Adonis*:

> Full gently now she takes him by the hand,
> A lily prison'd in a gaol of snow,
> Or ivory in an alabaster band:
> So white a friend engirts so white a foe.

His point is that, in this account of two sorts of whiteness, the elements of the metaphors remain separate entities, although yoked together by the lines: *lily, snow; ivory, alabaster; white friend, white foe.* There is no *interaction*, no blending of the elements here: the boundaries between them remain intact. In other words, the passage lacks Imagination,

> . . . the power by which one image or feeling is made to modify many others, and by a sort of fusion to force many into one . . . combining many circumstances into one moment of thought to produce that ultimate end of human thought and human feeling, unity, and thereby the reduction of the spirit to its principle and fountain, who alone is truly *One*.
>
> *(Coleridge on Shakespeare*, pp. 64–5)

As he says elsewhere,

> . . . images, however beautiful, though faithfully copied from nature, and as accurately represented in words, do not of themselves characterize the poet. They become proofs of original genius only as far as they are modified by a predominant passion; or by associated thoughts or images awakened by that passion; or when they have the effect of reducing multitude to unity, or succession to an instant. . .
>
> *(Biographia Literaria*, Chap. XV)

As an example of this imaginative process, and of the unity produced by 'this greatest faculty of the human mind' he cites this metaphor from the same poem:

> Look! how a bright star shooteth from the sky;
> So glides he in the night from Venus' eye!
>
> (ll. 815–16)

– and it is easy to see what he is getting at. In his own words,

> How many images and feelings are here brought together without effort and without discord, in the beauty of Adonis, the rapidity of his flight, the yearning, yet hopelessness of the enamoured gazer, and a shadowy ideal character is thrown over the whole.
>
> *(Coleridge on Shakespeare*, p. 65)

What he means is that each element of the metaphor interacts with each other element: each affects and is affected by the other, and the result is unity. As I. A. Richards says of these lines,

> The separable meanings of each word, *Look*! (our surprise at the meteor, hers at his flight), *star* (a light-giver, an influence, a remote and uncontrollable thing) *shooteth* (the sudden, irremediable, portentous fall or death of what had been a guide, a destiny), *the sky* (the source of light and now of ruin), *glides* (not rapidity only, but fatal ease too), *in the night* (the darkness of the scene and of Venus' world now) – all these separable meanings are here brought into one.
>
> (*Coleridge on Imagination*, p. 83)

Not only do we sense the way in which Adonis's flight appeared to Venus, but we also find ourselves, because of the inter-connections on which the metaphor insists, *creatively* and sympathetically making these connections ourselves. Instead (as in the case of Fancy's metaphor) of being confronted by clever comparisons, whose precisely worked-out relations we passively contemplate, this metaphor gives us work to do. The pattern of thought it proposes is, as it were, referred from Shakespeare's mind to our own, and requires our participation to 'complete' it. It draws us in, involves us in its own process, gives us the responsibility for the creative act of *closure* with itself. This vitalizes the metaphor. As Coleridge says, in one of his many brilliantly illuminating comments on Shakespeare, 'You feel him to be a poet, inasmuch as for a time he has made you one – an active creative being.'

The distinction between metaphors of the Fancy and those of the Imagination is a valuable one, for it begins to suggest a means of analysing metaphor in terms rather more appropriate to itself than those of Aristotle and his followers. Their analysis took account only of the relationship of the metaphor's elements to each other. Coleridge seems to want to take into account the relationship between the metaphor and its audience, on the grounds that the degree of imaginative response of those to whom the metaphor is addressed contributes in full measure to its final effect.

Let us now return to the terms *abstract* and *concrete*, and briefly glance at them in relation to Fancy and Imagination themselves, and in a context which makes Coleridge's constant use of Shakespeare as an example a matter of considerable significance. The central feature of the metaphors of Fancy is that they do not creatively involve their audience in themselves. They are 'abstract' in this sense and, however ingenious they may be, there is a gulf between them and their audience which matches and reflects the gulf between the separate elements which compose them. They are metaphors in which the language is used selfconsciously, artificially. They are metaphors, in effect, characteristic of language in a particular form. That is, when it is written down.

The metaphors which spring from the Imagination do, as has been said, require the involvement of an audience. In this sense, they are part of 'concrete' experience, and their language is never self-conscious, or artificial. Indeed, as Coleridge says, the Imagination

> acts by so carrying on the eye of the reader as to make him almost lose the consciousness of words – to make him *see* everything, as Wordsworth has grandly and appropriately said,
>
> > *Flashed* upon that inward eye
> > Which is the bliss of solitude;
>
> – and to make everything present by a series of images. And this without exciting any painful or laborious attention, without any *anatomy* of description ... but with the sweetness and easy movement of nature.
>
> (*Coleridge on Shakespeare*, p. 66)

Language, Coleridge claimed, is the 'armoury of the human mind', containing the 'weapons of its future conquests'. What seemed to him lacking in the previous century and in his own was a proper sense of language's power, in its capacity as an instrument of the Imagination, to conquer a realm beyond the immediate world perceived by the eye. We live, he claimed, under a 'despotism of the eye' from which Plato had aimed to emancipate us. But nevertheless,

> under this strong sensuous influence, we are restless because invisible things are not the objects of vision; and metaphysical systems, for the most part, become popular, not for their truth, but in proportion as they attribute to causes a susceptibility of being seen, if only our visual organs were sufficiently powerful.
>
> (Biographia Literaria, Chap. VI)

It is exactly this 'susceptibility of being seen' that is the standard applied by Dr Johnson to Shakespeare's metaphor of Duncan's 'silver skin laced with his golden blood'. By that standard, the metaphor is indeed improper. It yields hardly anything to the sight, and minds accustomed, by their very commitment to literacy, to the visual modes of reading and writing as the most rewarding forms of communication will find its elements wholly unrelated to each other, and thus incomprehensible. In 'abstract' visual terms, under the despotism of the eye, such a metaphor does not and cannot work.

But the Imagination, by its nature, is directed towards that *inward* eye that Wordsworth celebrates. And the language appropriate to its nature can for that reason hardly be language in written form. For whilst writing offers a physical counterpart of language, it is not its primary mode of communication. Language's 'concrete' and primary form is speech, human utterance. And far from reproducing speech, writing could be said to *reduce* it. Writing takes the full resonance of oral utterance, imbued as it is with the personality, tone of voice and bodily presence of its speaker, from whom it is never normally separated, and replaces these with the impersonality and silence of marks on paper. The richness of oral ambiguity, of the 'language really used by men', is replaced by the relatively antiseptic and certainly abstract 'clarity' of writing, where each word's 'meaning' can be precisely assigned. Dr Johnson was a great *writer* (and a very great compiler of dictionaries which assign 'meaning'). In his view 'A dramatic exhibition is a *book* recited with concomitants that increase or diminish its effect' (*Preface to Shakespeare*, 1765). However, Shakespeare's medium was the *oral* dimension of the language. Most of his audience was probably non-literate. And in any case, he was a *dramatist*, not a writer. As drama, as utterance, the metaphor of Duncan's 'silver' skin and 'golden' blood works very well indeed. As Coleridge said 'poetry gives most pleasure when only generally and not perfectly understood'. I. A. Richards comments on this that 'what he is pointing to is the superiority of the characteristic Shakespearean structure of meaning over the characteristic later eighteenth century structures' (*op. cit.*, p. 215).

This is not the place to argue whether it was this oral aspect of Shakespeare's 'structure of meaning' that most appealed to the romantic mind. But it is worth pointing out that the sort of metaphors Coleridge assigned to the Imagination are those which exhibit the most obvious characteristics of speech. The interaction of the elements, the 'esemplastic' fusing together of the parts, are the sorts of things that happen, naturally, when we speak; especially if we are driven by the 'spontaneous overflow of powerful feelings'. As Marshall McLuhan has described it, in oral interchange

> there are numerous simultaneous vistas of any topic whatever. The subject is looked at swiftly from many angles: classic notions and insights concerning that subject are, via memory, on the tip of every tongue in the intimate group.

– whereas, in respect of the written word,

> The reader's eye not only prefers one sound, one tone, in isolation; it prefers one meaning at a time. Simultaneities like puns and ambiguities – the life of spoken discourse – become, in writing, affronts to taste, floutings of efficiency.
> ('The Effect of the Printed Book on Language in the 16th Century')

In short, Coleridge's idea of the Imagination and the way in which it differs from the Fancy, leads us directly to language, and to the spoken language at that; its greatest artist Shakespeare. The notion of Fancy leads, almost as directly, to a language 'reduced' to its isolated elements, each with its 'meaning' carefully and separately defined. In a sense, and certainly to Coleridge, the 'model' for this sort of language is Hartley's doctrine of the association of ideas. Words, like ideas, are 'associated' with each other in the way that bricks are brought together to build up a wall. Each word has a carefully established relationship to a Thing which it represents, physically (Swift had neatly satirized exactly this notion of language in his own day in *Gulliver's Travels* where the scientists in Laputa hold objects up to each other as a substitute for talking).

It is this artificial distinction between language and reality, words and things, that Coleridge's idea of Imagination is designed to break down. 'I would', he wrote to Godwin in September 1800, 'endeavour to destroy the old antithesis of Words and Things: elevating, as it were Words into Things and living Things too.'

Metaphor provides the means by which words are 'elevated' into 'living Things', because for a word to 'live' it needs to be uttered, or at least to feel utterable; to have the impress of 'real men' upon it. The poet, Wordsworth reminds us, is ' a man speaking to men'. And when metaphor reduces 'multitude to unity, or succession to an instant', it is doing what the speaking voice does with language: imposing the unity of a single personality on the multitudinousness of sound, and substituting the immediacy of utterance for the silent sequential process of writing and reading. Thus, '. . . images, however beautiful' only become 'proofs of original genius' when 'a human and intellectual life is transferred to them from the poet's own spirit'. So, the following metaphor, whilst not objectionable, remains merely mechanical, and would not be out of place 'in a book of topography':

> Behold yon row of pines, that shorn and bowed
> Bend from the sea-blast, seen at twilight eve.

But when the same metaphor is slightly modified, invested and merged with humanity, it rises 'into semblance of poetry':

> Yon row of bleak and visionary pines,
> By twilight glimpse discerned, mark! how they flee
> From the fierce sea-blast, all their tresses wild
> Streaming before them.

> (*Biographia Literaria*, Chap. XV)

'Language,' says Coleridge, 'is framed to convey not the object alone, but likewise the character, mood and intentions of the person who is representing it.' Language, that is, is utterance: it utters (or 'outers') the inner reality and, by Imagination, imposes this on the world beyond. By this means (and it is a process, as we shall see, that has occupied the attention of modern linguists and anthropologists) language and 'reality' are intimately related.

Nature, the 'prime genial artist', is also involved in a process of 'completion', of blending and fusing variety into unity. So man's art imitates nature by imitating this process. His Imagination, as the faculty which blends and fuses, is thus 'a repetition in the finite mind of the eternal act of creation'.

Imagination, then, is the 'shaping spirit' that projects man's mind onto the world, making it interact with the world, as the elements of metaphor interact with each other. 'Reality' is thus the product of the Imagination and that upon which it plays. Its most obvious manifestation is linguistic and, as Coleridge wrote to James Gillman in 1827, in terms that reveal the full extent of his opposition to the view of language promulgated by Sprat,

It is the fundamental mistake of grammarians and writers on the philosophy of grammar and language to suppose that words and their syntaxis are the immediate representatives of *things*, or that they correspond to *things*. Words correspond to thoughts, and the legitimate order and connection of words to the *laws* of thinking and to the acts and affections of the thinker's mind.

He adds, perhaps sensing the inadequacy even of his own writing, '... Read this over till you understand it. God bless you.'

Imagination stretches the mind, then, because it 'stretches' reality by the linguistic means of metaphor. Given this, metaphor cannot be thought of as simply a cloak for a pre-existing thought. A metaphor *is* a thought in its own right.

There is, finally, no way in which language can be 'cleared' of metaphor. Even Sprat's own pronouncements against 'swellings' of style, and in favour of a way of speaking that is 'close' and 'naked' are themselves riddled with metaphorical transferences of an obvious kind. Style can only 'swell' metaphorically, and this is the only way in which speech can be 'close' and 'naked'. Language may attempt to come 'near the Mathematical plainness', but it can only do so by means of a metaphor of proximity in spatial relationships that itself is far from plain, and far from Mathematics.

We live in a world of metaphors of the world, out of which we construct myths. We make the world up, in other words, as we go along, and we experience it concretely. Only if we are mistaken do we

> think of ourselves as separate beings, and place nature in antithesis to the mind, as object to subject, thing to thought, death to life. This is abstract knowledge, or the science of the mere understanding.

Concrete knowledge, on the other hand, recognizes that

> the finite form can neither be laid hold of, nor is it anything of itself real, but merely an apprehension, a framework which the human imagination forms by its own limits, as the foot measures itself on the snow.

> > (*The Friend*, 2 ii, 1818)

It is of the essence of the Romantic revolution to have stressed the concrete links between man and the natural world. Coleridge, in giving these links an indelible linguistic stamp, thereby places metaphor at the centre of human concern, making it something far more important than an object of idle speculation for classifying literary critics. The words of perhaps his greatest interpreter, I. A. Richards, indicate the scope of this achievement:

> Because all objects which we can name or otherwise single out . . . are projections of man's interests; because the Universe as it is known to us is a fabric whose forms, as we alone can know them, have arisen in and through reflection; and because that reflection, whether made by the intellect in science or by 'the whole soul of man' in poetry, has developed through language – and apart from language, can neither be continued nor maintained – the study of the modes of language becomes, as it attempts to be thorough, the most fundamental and extensive of all enquiries . . . Thus the more traditional subjects of criticism, Coleridge's differentiation of imagination from fancy, and his still abstruser ponderings on objectification and the living word, unite with the analysis of the ambiguities and confusions that are overt or latent in all cases of metaphor, transference or projection to form one study . . . With Coleridge we step across the threshold of a general theoretical study of language capable of opening to us new powers over our minds.

(Coleridge on Imagination, pp. 231–2)

5

Some Twentieth Century Views

> Reality is a cliché from which we escape by metaphor
> (Wallace Stevens)

The twentieth century has of course produced more than one 'general theoretical study of language capable of opening to us new powers over our minds'. And in general, modern literary criticism, linguistics and anthropology have maintained and reinforced the essentials of the Coleridgean or Romantic revolution: the dissolution of the artificial barrier between human nature and 'nature', thought and 'thing', language and the 'real' world. What Coleridge calls 'abstract' knowledge, or 'the science of the mere understanding', deriving from the illusion that man perceives and experiences the world objectively, and can therefore, in abstraction, measure and assess 'reality' whilst distancing himself from it, has been challenged by the notion that the only genuine knowledge is of a more 'concrete' sort, arising from 'lived' and personalized experience, in a world whose 'reality' is really an extremely relative matter.

I. A. RICHARDS

In the event, it has proved to be I. A. Richards himself who perhaps more than any other has seen the importance of the role any account of language's function in society must assign to metaphor. His arguments in *The Philosophy of Rhetoric* (1936) grow to a considerable extent out of those of Coleridge and of Vico, and they constitute a formidable and formative statement on the subject of metaphor which has had a radical influence in the modern world.

He starts from the proposition that all 'meanings' are universally relative, only appropriate to and valid in the cultural context in which they occur:

> ... any part of a discourse, in the last resort, does what it does only because the other parts of the surrounding, uttered or unuttered discourse, and its conditions, are what they are.
>
> (*The Philosophy of Rhetoric*, p. 10.)

Thus 'meaning' is not a stable or 'fixed' quality, but one which words or groups of words acquire in use. Just as human beings 'create' reality (so-called) by imposing concepts of 'things' onto what the philosopher A. N. Whitehead saw as 'merely the hurrying of material, endlessly, meaninglessly', so we impose 'meanings' covertly and without being aware of the process on sounds that, in themselves, have no 'objective' or 'real' meaning.

Language, on this showing, is emphatically *not* the 'dress' of thought; that is, the medium through which we communicate to each other information about a reality that already exists in the 'real world' outside us. On the contrary, language *causes* that reality to exist, so that

> We shall do better to think of a meaning as though it were a plant that has grown – not a can that has been filled or a lump of clay that has been moulded.
>
> (*Ibid.* p. 12)

Words, it follows, are not *events* in themselves, so much as the totality of the *conventions* which derive from our employment of them. *Words* do not 'mean'; *we* 'mean' *by* words. The total fabric of our 'meanings' – which constitutes 'the world' as we know it – consists not of actual or inherited experience, 'revived duplicates of individual past impressions' each attached to an appropriate word or set of words, but of linguistic and psychological 'laws' regarding 'recurrent likenesses of behaviour in our minds and in the world' to which words are variously adapted by us. Any passage of language can thus hardly have only *one* meaning appropriate to it (and Richards pours considerable scorn on the 'One and Only One True Meaning Superstition').

In short, this 'theorem' suggests and requires that *ambiguity*, sometimes thought of as a 'vice' of language, the cause of 'breakdown' or misunderstanding in communication, be redefined and recognized as a fundamental and necessary aspect of language; part of its equipment which may be developed to further, deepen, or enrich 'meaning'. Such a view (p. 40)

> . . . will make us expect ambiguity to the widest extent and of the subtlest kinds nearly everywhere . . . But where the old Rhetoric treated ambiguity as a fault in language, and hoped to confine or eliminate it, the new Rhetoric sees it as an inevitable consequence of the powers of language and as the indispensable means of most of our most important utterances – especially in Poetry and Religion.

To put it another way, the 'new Rhetoric' virtually asserts with the Romantics that speech, with its inherently ambiguous nature, is language's primary and defining form, after two centuries of the domination of language's secondary and derived form, with its opposite goals of clarity and distinctiveness, writing.

This is also the point from which much modern linguistic analysis of language starts. Man is seen as the talking animal. Speech is his distinctive feature, and it is language that marks him off from the other animals. Accordingly, his encounters with the world take place within a predominantly linguistic context. And as a result, his experience of the world is modified by the structure of his language. His language is an organic, self-contained, autonomous system which divides and classifies experience in its own terms and along its own lines. In the course of the process it imposes its own particular 'shape' on the world of those who speak it. In effect, then, language and experience interact and prove fundamentally implicated with each other to an extent that makes it difficult to consider them as separate entities. A language 'creates' reality in its own image. To use language thus essentially involves 'getting at' one kind of reality 'through' another. The process is fundamentally one of 'transference'.

More will be said on this subject later, but for the moment we might note the extent to which this view in general supports and confirms the Romantic opposition to the idea that metaphor involves a 'special' and 'out of the ordinary' use of language. *All* language, by the nature of its 'transferring' relation to 'reality' described above, is fundamentally metaphorical. Metaphor, as Richards says, is not something special and exceptional in the use of language, some kind of 'deviation from its normal mode of working'. Nor is its prime concern the mere making of verbal pictures; 'We cannot too firmly recognize that how a figure of speech works has nothing necessarily to do with how any images, as copies or duplicates of sense perceptions may, for reader or writer, be backing up his words.' Metaphor is a function of *language*, not of picture-making. It is not simply '. . . something to do with the presence of images, in the mind's eye or the mind's ear'. On the contrary, it is the 'omni-present principle' of all language. Indeed, all languages contain deeply embedded metaphorical structures which covertly influence overt 'meaning'. A language cannot be 'cleared' of metaphor without using a metaphor in the verb 'to clear'. No use of language can be 'straightforward', that is free of metaphor, since it will make use of metaphor even while making that claim (here, the sense of direct purposeful undeviating movement in a particular direction through space, 'transferred' to a way of speaking or writing). Metaphor, in short, is the way language works.

More particularly, it involves a certain linguistic process:

In the simplest formulation, when we use a metaphor we have two thoughts of different things active together and supported by a single word, or phrase, whose meaning is a resultant of their interaction.

(*op. cit.*, p. 93)

'Interaction' is the significant word here. Richards distinguishes the elements involved as the 'tenor' (or the 'general drift', the underlying idea which the metaphor expresses) and the 'vehicle' (the basic analogy which is used to embody or carry the tenor). Thus, in Matthew Arnold's metaphor,

> Yes: in the sea of life enisl'd,
> With echoing straits between us thrown,
> Dotting the shoreless watery wild,
> We mortal millions live *alone*.

> (*To Marguerite*)

the *tenor* is the way of life of people living alone, the *vehicle* the islands separated from each other by the sea. These elements interact, and their 'transaction' generates the only genuine 'meaning' of the metaphor:

> the co-presence of the vehicle and tenor results in a meaning (to be clearly distinguished from the tenor) which is not attainable *without* their interaction.

> (*op. cit.*, p. 100.)

The vehicle, he adds 'is not normally mere embellishment of a tenor which is otherwise unchanged by it but . . . vehicle and tenor in co-operation give a meaning of more varied powers than can be ascribed to either.'

We have already noticed that the term 'interaction' applies equally to the working at large of language itself. The 'meaning' of a language for the people who speak it results from and lies in the interaction which takes place between their language and their experience. Each modifies the other, and their 'co-presence' generates 'reality' as they know it. The process is 'vitally metaphorical'.

So metaphor is hardly an amusing embellishment or diversion, an 'escape' from the harsh realities of life or of language. It is made out of, *and it makes* those realities. Their 'opposite and discordant' qualities are given, by metaphor's interactive function, a form and an integrity, a role and an order. In this sense, man's reality is formed by the metaphorical processes that inform his language.

And so Richards quite properly takes to task the poet and philosopher T. E. Hulme for his distinction, to which we have already referred, between language and reality in poetry. Hulme says that

> Plain speech is essentially inaccurate. It is only by new metaphors . . . that it can be made precise.

Hence poetry (and so metaphor)

> is a compromise for a language of intuition which would hand over sensations bodily. It always endeavours to arrest you, and make you continuously see a physical thing, to prevent you gliding through an abstract process. It chooses fresh epithets and fresh metaphors, not so much because they are new, and we are tired of the old, but because the old cease to convey a physical thing and become abstract counters.
>
> (*Speculations* pp. 134–5)

The notion that there exists a 'reality' of bodily sensations separate from the language in which these can be described is systematically misleading. It asserts a distinction between language and experience which can hardly be upheld, and has the effect, to which Richards rightly objects, of claiming for 'poetic' language in general, and for metaphor in particular, a 'special' and visually 'accurate' picture-making quality supposedly denied to 'plain speech'.

In any case, language is far from being a *substitute* for real experience. In fact, as has been said, by articulating the experience it *constitutes* it:

> Words are the meeting points at which regions of experience which can never combine in sensation or intuition come together. They are the occasion and the means of that growth which is the mind's endless endeavour to order itself. That is why we have language. It is no mere signalling system. It is the instrument of all our distinctively human development, of everything in which we go beyond the other animals.
>
> (*op. cit.*, p. 131.)

Language, in short, does not simply *report* things. It makes things happen.

Given this, the chief use of metaphor, Richards recognized, is to *extend* language and, since language is reality, to expand reality. By the juxtaposition of elements whose interaction brings about a new dimension for them both, metaphor can reasonably be said to create *new* reality, and to secure that reality within the language, where it is accessible to the people who speak it.

Accordingly, language '. . . is utterly unable to aid us except through the command of metaphor which it gives', and this is why Aristotle, as we have already noted, argued that a command of metaphor is 'by far the most important thing to master', and 'the mark of great natural ability'.

WILLIAM EMPSON

This places the poet, of course, in the position in which the Romantics saw him, at the frontiers of reality as far as his culture is concerned. He, by his conscious use of metaphor, is actively engaged in a 'stretching' process whereby new areas of reality are constantly enclosed in the language, new dimensions of experience recorded, and made available within its confines.

Such 'stretching' of the language means that 'stability' in the area of meaning will not be something with which a poet will be overly concerned, and Richards' best-known pupil, William Empson, has contributed an important essay on exactly this topic, in his *Seven Types of Ambiguity* (1930) which strongly reinforces the notion that ambiguity is the necessary aspect of language enabling the process of metaphor to operate most fruitfully. As he puts it:

> An ambiguity, in ordinary speech, means something very pronounced, and as a rule witty or deceitful. I propose to use the word in an extended sense, and shall think relevant to my subject any verbal nuance, however slight, which gives room for alternative reactions to the same piece of language.
>
> (*2nd. edition*, p. 1)

It is ultimately ambiguity in this 'extended' sense which makes metaphor possible. If each word has only a single (or One True) 'meaning', then the 'meaning' of one word can in no way be affected by or 'transferred' to another, nor could new 'meanings' be generated simply by juxtaposing one word with another. 'Ambiguity' implies a dynamic quality in language which enables meaning to be deepened and enriched as various 'layers' of it become simultaneously available;

> ... what often happens when a piece of writing is felt to offer hidden riches is that one phrase after another lights up and appears as the heart of it; one part after another catches fire ...
>
> (*op. cit.*, p. xi)

'All good poetry', Empson argues, is ambiguous in this sense. It contains 'a feeling of generalisation from a case which has been presented definitely'.

Empson's concept of metaphor differs from that of Richards to the extent that the clear-cut distinction between tenor and vehicle can hardly be maintained when the number of 'possible' meanings offered by any metaphor expands, without any of them becoming necessarily dominant over the others, and thus discernible as 'tenor'. His major contribution is to recognize that ambiguity is inherently a characteristic of language, and that metaphor is fundamentally part of the same process '... because metaphor, more or less far-fetched, more or less complicated, more or less taken for granted (so as to be unconscious), is the normal mode of development of a language'. From this, it becomes possible to argue that in the use it makes of metaphor's multiple 'ambiguities', poetry in fact exploits the central characteristic of language itself.

OWEN BARFIELD, PHILIP WHEELWRIGHT

The notion that language is by nature fundamentally meta-phorical in mode, and thus potentially 'ambiguous' in content has proved to be a fruitful and a central one for many modern writers on the subject.

Owen Barfield found that the metaphorical process was in fact, in the form of what he called 'tarning' [from the German word *Tarnung* meaning to say one thing and mean another] to be found 'everywhere in language', not just in 'officially' designated metaphors. It was a necessary linguistic process to which a man must resort in the field of law as much as in that of poetry;

> If therefore he would say anything really new, if that which was hitherto unconscious is to become conscious, he must resort to tarning. He must talk what is nonsense on the face of it, but in such a way that the recipient may have the new meaning suggested to him. This is the true importance of metaphor.
>
> ('Poetic Diction and Legal Fiction' in *Essays Presented to Charles Williams*)

Philip Wheelwright, in his studies *The Burning Fountain* (1954) and *Metaphor and Reality* (1962), also finds metaphor at the centre of language, and indeed constructs a definition of language so as to bring out and reinforce metaphor's *modus operandi*, of 'getting at' one thing 'through' another:

> In this broadest possible sense of the word 'language' I mean to designate any element in human experience which is not merely contemplated for its own sake alone, but is employed to *mean*, to *intend*, to *stand proxy for* something beyond itself.
>
> (*Metaphor and Reality* p. 29)

Indeed, so concerned are critics like Barfield and Wheelwright to stress this 'tarning' aspect of metaphor, they are content largely to ignore many of the old rhetorical distinctions, particularly that between metaphor and simile. Barfield, arguing that the 'essential nature of figurative language . . . is most clearly apparent in the figure called metaphor' is prepared to call a long and elaborate metaphor 'a simile with the word "like" missed out'. This breezy and unrigid use of terms is worth quoting in full:

The language of poetry has always been in a high degree *figurative*; it is always illustrating or expressing what it wishes to put before us by comparing that with something else. Sometimes the comparison is open and avowed, as when Shelley compares the skylark to a poet, to a high-born maiden, and to a rose embowered in its own green leaves; when Keats tells us that a summer's day is

> like the passage of an angel's tear
> That falls through the clear ether silently,

or when Burns writes simply: 'My love is like a red red rose.' And then we call it a 'simile'. Sometimes it is concealed in the form of a bare statement, as when Shelley says of the west wind, not that it is *like*, but that it *is* 'the breath of Autumn's being', calls upon it to 'make him its lyre' and says of himself that *his* leaves are falling. This is known as 'metaphor'. Sometimes the element of comparison drops still farther out of sight. Instead of saying that A is like B or that A is B, the poet simply talks about B, without making any overt reference to A at all. You know, however, that he intends A all the time, or, better say that you know he intends *an* A; for you may not have a very clear idea of what A is and even if you have got an idea, somebody else may have a different one. This is generally called 'symbolism'.

(op. cit., p. 107.)

Wheelwright no less authoritatively urges 'that the grammarian's familiar distinction between metaphor and simile is to be largely ignored' (*Metaphor and Reality,* p. 71), pointing out that Burns' line 'My love is like a red, red rose' is grammatically a simile, and yet has far more 'metaphoric vitality' than, say, 'Love is a red rose' which would be grammatically a metaphor. He is even prepared to discount words like 'image' and 'symbol' as tending to prejudice one's attitude towards, and one's theory of poetry. And he concludes that 'the test of essential metaphor is not any rule of grammatical form, but rather the quality of semantic transformation that is brought about' (p. 71). In fact, he goes on to suggest a classification of metaphor in terms of the *mode* of 'semantic transformation' manifested in the process (as distinct from Richards' use of 'tenor' and 'vehicle' to describe the *units* involved), and coins two terms which describe the major structural qualities of each: *'epiphor'* 'standing for the outreach and extension of meaning through comparison' and *'diaphor'* 'the creation of new meaning by juxtaposition and synthesis'. A simple example of *epiphor* would be 'the milk of human kindness', where human kindness is 'compared' to milk, with its suggestion of blandness, sustenance, mother–child relationship etc. An example of *diaphor* would be Ezra Pound's disturbing juxtaposition:

> The apparition of these faces in the crowd;
> Petals on a wet, black bough.

And of course, some metaphors effectively combine both *epiphor* and *diaphor*.

CHRISTINE BROOKE-ROSE

That the process of metaphor is located at the heart of language and indeed defines and refines it, and thus man himself, remains the central stance of most twentieth-century writers on the subject, and their overriding preoccupation. It is one which often tends to find itself opposed to scrupulous analysis on these very grounds. John Middleton Murry argues that

> Metaphor is as ultimate as speech itself, and speech is as ultimate as thought. If we try to penetrate them beyond a certain point, we find ourselves questioning the very faculty and instrument with which we are trying to penetrate them.
>
> (*Countries of the Mind*, 1931)

Of course, this view begs many questions, and it is only another way of putting it to suggest that such questioning is a valuable exercise, in that the analysis of metaphor offers a very good way of probing the nature of languages and the ways of life which derive from them.

In any case, there have been successful approaches to metaphor in recent years whose specific and achieved object has been a considerable and valuable degree of linguistic 'penetration'. In particular, one might mention Christine Brooke-Rose's *A Grammar of Metaphor* (1958).

The very terms of grammatical ordering in which such a study is cast, the very end of analysis by parts of speech which it sets itself, may seem oppressive, and obviously limited. But Miss Brooke-Rose's concern is primarily to dispel mystery by simply exploring the implications of the obvious fact that 'metaphor is expressed in words, and a metaphoric word reacts on other words to which it is syntactically and grammatically related' (p. 1).

Following a lead which had been vigorously established in another connection a few years earlier by Donald Davie's study of syntax in poetry, *Articulate Energy* (1955), Miss Brooke-Rose engages in much valuable analysis of the difference, for instance, between the use of transitive and intransitive verbs in metaphor and the use of the copula construction (the verb 'to be') as a means of linking its elements. She convincingly explodes the fallacy that the transitive verb is inherently superior to the intransitive, and finds the copula more commonly used among great writers than some stylistic critics would have us suppose.

Her major interest of course lies in the grammatical structure of metaphor, and not in its content or its relationship to reality. Metaphor, she insists

> is not merely the perception of similarity in dissimilarity, it is the changing of words by one another, and syntax is rich in methods of doing this. . .
>
> (*A Grammar of Metaphor*, p. 93.)

Her book provides an exhaustive and systematic analysis of the use of nouns, verbs and other parts of speech, in those methods.

The five main categories of Noun metaphors she details are:

1. *Simple Replacement*, in which the metaphor's proper term is replaced, and thus has to be inferred by the reader.

2. *The Pointing Formulae*, in which the proper term A is mentioned, then replaced by the metaphor B with some demonstrative expression 'pointing' back to the proper term.

3. *The Copula*, a direct statement that A is B which can also include more 'timid or cautious terms' such as 'to seem', 'to call', 'to become', etc.

4. *The Link with 'To Make'*, a direct statement involving a third party: C *makes* A into B.

5. *The Genitive Link*, in which the vehicle or noun metaphor is linked by 'of' to the tenor, or to a third term, not necessarily the obvious tenor: thus B is part of, or derives from, or belongs to C, from which relationship we can infer A. E.g. 'the hostel of my heart' as a metaphor for the body.

For all the accuracy, and occasionally the ingenuity of such an analysis, the question of its usefulness remains crucial. Does a knowledge of these categories help us in our responses to poetry, over and above the information it offers about the way metaphors may be constructed in English? The very distinctions between the categories can come to seem unreal when a poem comes into view. Or, perhaps, they engage the mind on a quite different level from that of the metaphors they purport to describe, and the transition between these levels is crucially difficult to effect. In any case, they are bound to treat metaphors out of context: that is, beyond the reach of those other factors – rhythm, rhyme, 'sound-effects' of all kinds, position in the poem, relationship with other metaphors, the status of items of vocabulary, and so on, all of which contribute to and are part of the metaphor as it *actually* occurs.

Inevitably, in trying to pursue what metaphor *does*, as opposed to what it *is*, we will find ourselves taken beyond the self-confessed limits of Miss Brooke-Rose's work. And as the study of metaphor is so closely involved with the study of language itself, we will have to enter what will probably turn out to have been among the most important fields of human inquiry in the twentieth century: those of linguistics and anthropology.

LINGUISTICS

Possibly the major contribution of modern linguistic studies to the question of metaphor lies in the area of the relationship of the language of poetry to 'ordinary' or 'standard' language. At bottom, the issue is that formulated by the Czech linguist Jan Mukařovský; 'Is poetic language a special brand of the standard, or is it an independent formation?' ('Standard Language and Poetic Language', p. 41). A linguist such as Henry Lee Smith feels strongly that the common ground between poetic and 'ordinary' language needs stressing, and will state as a 'basic assumption', necessary before any appropriate investigation into the 'literary' use of language can begin, that

> The spoken language and other systems used in oral communication underlie and are basic to all literary compositions. This means that the poet is first a speaker of his native language and the reader or hearer of his work has internalized the same linguistic system as the author. In other words, the poet cannot *write* anything that will be at variance with the rules, phonological and grammatical, of the spoken language.
> (Introduction to Epstein & Hawkes, *Linguistics and English Prosody*)

Wordsworth's commitment to 'the language really spoken by men' will come to mind here, as will the views of Shelley, Coleridge, and post-Romantic critics such as I. A. Richards.

Winifred Nowottny (who, whilst a critic rather than a professional linguist has a considerable and informed interest in language) begins with more or less the same 'basic assumptions' as Henry Lee Smith, together with an awareness of an 'increasing *rapprochement* between the interests of linguists and the interests of literary critics'. In her excellent study *The Language Poets Use* (1962) she finds that if the 'greatest of all the obstacles' between reader and poem '... is the notion of a "poetic diction" differing primarily in its vocabulary from the usages of ordinary life, the next in order of obfuscating power is preoccupation with metaphor' (p. viii). Metaphor, she thinks it important to remember, is a 'linguistic phenomenon', and the linguistic devices used by poets are essentially an exploration and an expansion of the potentialities of the language used by everybody. Smith had been prepared to allow that there were in language 'special conventions that are purely literary', but Mrs Nowottny defines 'literary' rather more closely. Since, in her view, the language of poetry is an *extension* of ordinary language, 'language at full stretch', then language is only specifically 'literary' in so far as it is 'stretched', concerned to operate on more than one level at the same time:

> a verbal structure is literary if it presents its topic at more than one level of presentation at the same time – or, alternatively, if one and the same utterance has more than one function in the structure of meaning in which it occurs.
>
> (p. 2)

And in this condition, of course, its essential character is metaphorical.

Metaphor, then, is one of the ways, and possibly the most important, in which the 'stretching' of language takes place. What happens in metaphor is that the 'literal' or 'dictionary' level at which words usually operate is systematically avoided, even violated. Metaphor conveys a relationship between two things by using a word or words *figuratively*, not literally; that is, in a special sense which is different from the sense it has in the contexts noted by the dictionary.

By contrast, in simile, words are used literally, or 'normally'. This thing A is said to be 'like' that thing, B. The description given to A and to B is as accurate as literal words can make it, and the reader is confronted by a kind of *fait accompli*, where sense-impressions are often the final test of success. Thus 'my car is like a beetle' uses the words 'car' and 'beetle' literally, and the simile depends for its success on the literal – even visual – accuracy of the comparison.

However, when a word is used figuratively, what is established is the expectation of some sort of imaginative 'linkage' with other words similarly used. Metaphor, by means of this sense of 'linkage' leads us towards the 'target' of its meaning, but does not 'contaminate', or predetermine that target for us, as simile does with its sense of *fait accompli*. Even in such a poor metaphor as 'my car beetles along' the reader is forced to make an imaginative 'completion' from within his own experience of what the metaphor figuratively suggests. There is, after all, no simple 'comparison' or 'analogy' made between the elements involved. In metaphor 'one constituent acts upon another almost like an X-ray'. The reader has to *do* something, to join in, in order to hit the 'target'.

The notion that metaphor requires a response, an act of 'completion' from the reader, almost as a play does from its audience, is one that we have, of course, met before. In fact, Coleridge's distinction between the operational modes of Fancy on the one hand and Imagination on the other is paralleled in Mrs Nowottny's distinction between simile and metaphor. In simile, as in Fancy, we have mere collocation, or in Coleridge's words 'the faculty of bringing together images dissimilar in the main by some one point or more of likeness distinguished'. In metaphor, we have the operation of the imagination, the 'esemplastic power' which, at its highest, involves the audience in the artist's creative act. In the case of Shakespeare, 'you feel him to be a poet, inasmuch as for a time he has made you one – an active creative being'.

Mrs Nowottny thus seems faithful to the Romantic tradition and, like her illustrious forebears, she reaches the conclusion that poetic language differs from 'standard' language not in kind, but only in degree. As she says, in words that Wordsworth would certainly have approved,

> the chief difference between language in poems and language outside poems is that the one is more highly structured than the other, and the more complex organization set up in poems makes it possible for the poet both to redress and to exploit various characteristics of language at large.
>
> (p. 72)

It is the nature of that 'structure', the extent of that 'degree' of difference from the 'standard' which has most concerned the linguistically inclined critic in the last decade.

The question of poetic 'deviation' from the 'normal' use of language has been examined by many linguists, notably Jan Mukařovský mentioned above, whose concept of 'foregrounding' (an English version of the term *aktualisace*) raises most of the issues. In his view,

> The function of poetic language consists in the maximum of foregrounding of the utterance . . . it is not used in the services of communication, but in order to place in the foreground the act of expression, the act of speech itself.
>
> ('Standard Language and Poetic Language', pp. 43–4)

Deviation or 'foregrounding' obviously depends a good deal upon an established 'norm' or 'background' which throws it into relief, and in the study of metaphor a central problem has been how to characterize the 'standard' structures from which a metaphor can be said to 'deviate'. It is an important matter to the extent that when a metaphor loses its 'deviant' character, and becomes part of 'standard' language, then it is said to be 'dead'. It ceases to be part of the 'foreground' and merges into the background, as in the case of a metaphor like 'the leg of the table'. 'Standard' language is hardly metaphor-less, but its metaphors have an inert quality which needs to be defined, and the poet has to have access to linguistic devices which indicate that those he constructs are by comparison to be taken as 'foreground' and alive.

Various linguistic methods have been applied to this issue (see the excellent survey by Seymour Chatman and S. R. Levin in their article 'Linguistics and Poetics' in *The Encyclopedia of Poetry and Poetics*) – and they have proved relevant in various degrees.

For instance, statistical 'counts' of the incidence of various kinds of combinations of words gathered from some corpus of 'normal' language will obviously provide a crude index of the extent to which any metaphor is overtly 'deviant' in terms of the relative rarity or frequency of its particular structure. The same process could also, and more easily, be applied to an individual poem, where the metaphorical 'norm' *within* the poem might be established statistically, and the degree of 'deviation' in some metaphors thereby computed. In a poem where the metaphor was 'normally' formed by, say, a transitive verb ('the ship ploughed the waves'), a metaphor formed adjectivally, or by means of the copula ('the ship was a plough through the waves') might be distinctly 'deviant'.

Information theory treats the question of deviation not in terms of frequency but, rather more interestingly, in terms of the *probability* of occurrence, based on an analysis of what 'normally' occurs. Thus, some co-occurrences of words in terms of potential metaphorical constructs, such as 'white' and 'snow', or 'ship' and 'plough', have a fairly high degree of probability in English. Others, such as 'pugilistic' and 'bicycle' obviously have a much lower one, although they *could* occur together in an adjective–noun construction. The notion of *lexis*, as a level of 'patterning' of which words are capable over and above the syntactic structures in which they exist, seems to be a fruitful one in this connection. J. R. Firth has suggested the concept of 'collocation' as a means of expressing the 'normal' probability of the co-occurrence of words within a span of utterance, and the difference between the combinations of 'ship' and 'plough' on the one hand, and 'pugilistic' and 'bicycle' on the other could be stated, to use the phraseology of Angus McIntosh ('Patterns and Ranges', *Language*, Vol. 37, No. 3, 1961) by saying that the latter combination does not exhibit the same 'potential of collocability' as the former. The words' 'ranges' do not normally include each other.

Obviously, this offers a means of assessing the extent to which a particular metaphor occupies 'foreground' or 'background'. In the case of a metaphor like 'the leg of the table', we would say that the collocation of 'leg' and 'table' had a fairly high degree of probability of occurrence. In the case, however, of T. S. Eliot's metaphor,

> Let us go then, you and I
> Where the evening is spread out against the sky
> Like a patient etherised upon a table,
> > (*The Love Song of J. Alfred Prufrock*)

the elements proposed for 'transference', *evening* and *patient*, *spread out* and *etherised*, *sky* and (operating) *table* have a much lower potential of collocation both as pairs and in the larger units of tenor (evening spread out against the sky) and vehicle (patient etherized upon a table). On the principle that the higher the degree of potential collocation the more this makes the metaphor part of the 'background', and the lower the degree the more this pushes the metaphor into the foreground, we could then say that Eliot's metaphor exhibits a considerable degree of 'foregrounding'. This could even, should anyone wish to do so, be positioned on an appropriately calibrated scale.

The modern concept of *generative* grammar which, being neither descriptive (that is, derived from an account of actual linguistic occurrences) nor prescriptive (derived from a set of presuppositions about what *ought* to occur in the language), but concerned to supply a set of 'rules' for generating all the sentences of the language, perhaps is able to be helpful in respect of metaphor.

Certainly it can measure deviations and, by means of the complex nature of its 'rules', determine the way in which the 'deviant' metaphor deviates. This method has been effectively and cleverly used by Samuel R. Levin in his essay 'Poetry and Grammaticalness'.

Moreover, the 'transformational' aspect of generative grammar, whereby sentences are 'transformed' from one grammatical shape to another by means of a discernible set of 'rules', enables relationships *between* metaphors to be noticed and categorized, and so regularities and similarities that lie below the surface can be brought out. The work of Christine Brooke-Rose in this field has already been mentioned, and to that should be added the sort of analysis offered in Geoffrey N. Leech's *A Linguistic Guide to English Poetry*, especially Chapter 9 in which 'rules of transference of meaning' are formulated which make useful distinctions between Metaphor, Simile, Synecdoche, and Metonymy. In his essay 'Linguistics and the Figures of Rhetoric', Leech also draws a valuable distinction between the metaphor superimposed on an 'ordinary' background (a Syntagmatic Figure) and that which exists rather as a 'gap in the established code – a *violation* of the predictable pattern' (a Paradigmatic Figure).

And yet there is something odd and perhaps fundamentally misleading about the notion of metaphor as an overt 'deviation' from the rules of language. It systematically denies something of value to 'ordinary' life and language, and there is a sense in which Mr Leech's injunction that 'to use figurative language in expounding tenor and vehicle is merely to multiply one's task by explaining one metaphor by another' partly gives the game away. Metaphor invades language at large, covertly rather than overtly. 'Tenor' and 'vehicle' are themselves covert metaphors because metaphor is the means by which normal language normally works. Moreover, the distinction between 'background' and 'foreground' is difficult to maintain in the case of metaphor since a good poet is going to achieve many of his effects by switching from one level to another.

The re-animation of 'dead' or 'background' metaphors is part and parcel of the poet's art, whereby he gives (to quote Mallarmé) *un sens plus pur aux mots de la tribu.*

The linguist who has argued most persuasively for metaphor's centrality in respect of language is undoubtedly Roman Jakobson. Writing about the linguistic problems of the disorder called *aphasia* (loss or impairment of the power to understand and to use speech), Jakobson records his observation that the two major component disorders ('similarity disorder' and 'contiguity disorder') seem to be strikingly related to the two basic rhetorical figures metaphor and metonymy (*Fundamentals of Language* pp. 69–96).

In Jakobson's view, the distinction between these figures is fundamental. Metaphor proposes a 'transferable' similarity or analogy between one entity (e.g. the movement of my car) and another which may be substituted for it (the movement of a beetle). In the case of metonymy the basis for the substitution is not similarity so much as sequence. The entity involved in the substitution is chosen because it is 'adjacent' to or 'contiguous' with the one it replaces: it 'follows on' in sequence from it. So, for 'The President of the United States' we can substitute 'where the President lives', with the result that 'The White House' can serve as an example of metonymy for the President. In the same fashion, 'hands' can stand for men, 'the crown' for the monarchy, 'a good table' for good food and so on.

Jakobson observed that in patients suffering from 'similarity disorder', there was a marked inability to deal in language's 'associative' relationships, such as the use of synonyms, or alternative words for the same object; i.e. the raw material of metaphor. However, in such patients the capacity to join parts of language together seemed to have been unimpaired and they were able to supply 'adjacent' words quite readily: they would substitute *fork* for knife, *table* for lamp, *smoke* for fire, etc. Meanwhile, in the patient suffering from 'contiguity disorder', the reverse situation pertained. The 'syntactical rules organizing words into higher units' were lost, and the patient's speech appeared to be largely confined to the substitution of words by 'similarities ... of a metaphoric nature' (pp. 85–6). It seems, Jakobson concluded, as if 'metaphor is alien to the similarity disorder, and metonymy to the contiguity disorder' (p. 90).

As a result of his observations, Jakobson felt able to propose that human language in fact operates in terms of two fundamental dimensions whose characteristics are crystallized in the rhetorical devices of metaphor and metonymy. In effect, Jakobson sees these as the defining modes of a two-fold process of selection and combination by whose means all linguistic signs are formed: 'the given utterance (message) is a *combination* of constituent parts (sentences, words, phonemes, etc.) *selected* from the repository of all possible constituent parts (the code)' (*Fundamentals of Language* p. 75). Thus messages are constructed by the interaction of a 'horizontal' movement, which combines words together, and a 'vertical' movement, which selects the particular words from the available inventory of the language. The combinative (or syntagmatic) process manifests itself in contiguity (one word being placed next to another) and its mode is *metonymic*. The selective (or associative) process manifests itself in similarity (one word of concept being 'like' another) and its mode is *metaphoric*. The two axes may be represented as follows:

Selective/Associative Dimension (metaphor)

Combinative/Syntagmatic Dimension (metonymy)

Both metaphor and metonymy can be sub-divided into other figures (simile is a type of metaphor, synecdoche a type of metonymy) but the distinction between them remains fundamental, because it reflects the fundamental dimensions of language itself.

When language is used poetically, Jakobson argues, it draws on both the selective and the combinative modes in order to promote *equivalence*: 'The poetic function of language projects the principle of equivalence from the axis of selection into the axis of combination' ('Closing Statement: Linguistics and Poetics' p. 358). Thus, when I say 'my car beetles along' I *select* 'beetles' from a storehouse of other possibilities and *combine* it with 'car' on the principle that this will make the car's movement and the insect's movement *equivalent*. This gives the message complexity. In Jakobson's words, 'similarity superimposed on contiguity imparts to poetry its thoroughgoing symbolic, multiplex, polysemantic essence' ('Closing Statement: Linguistics and Poetics' p. 370).

However, it is worth remembering that poetry does not usually manifest itself in these abstract terms and neither do its metaphors. The 'meaning', value, and simple *existence* of any metaphor is discernible only as it actually occurs. And then it is properly perceived only in terms of its relationship with its entire context, that is, the other linguistic elements in the poem. In any context, any metaphor will be modified by such considerations as rhythmic quality, the syncopation between that and the overt 'meaning' of the words, the effect of rhyme or of the absence of rhyme, the position of the metaphor in the poem, in the line, even, in terms of its relative 'modernity' or archaic qualities, in time itself. The trouble with much modern linguistic analysis of metaphor is that it does not (and perhaps cannot) take into account the *full* context involved – and ultimately that would include the living human voice and *persona*. Yet language has no existence beyond these. As the anthropologist Claude Lévi-Strauss writes,

> ... language does not consist in the analytical reason of the old-style grammarians nor in the dialectic constituted by structural linguistics ... Language, an unreflecting totalization, is human reason which has its reasons and of which man knows nothing. And if it is objected that it is so only for a subject who internalizes it on the basis of linguistic theory, my reply is that this way out must be refused, for this subject is one who *speaks*: for the same light which reveals the nature of language to him also reveals to him that it was so when he did not know it, for he already made himself understood, and that it will remain so tomorrow without his being aware of it, since his discourse never was and never will be the result of a conscious totalization of linguistic laws.
>
> (*The Savage Mind*, p. 252)

ANTHROPOLOGY

The field of anthropology is essentially one in which the 'unreflecting' way people talk is related to the way they live. In fact, the close relationship between 'way of talking' and 'way of life', between language and culture, was a major concern of the American linguists B. L. Whorf and Edward Sapir. As Sapir says, making a point that has been referred to earlier,

> Language is guide to 'social reality' ... Human beings do not live in the objective world alone, nor alone in the world of social activity as ordinarily understood, but are very much at the mercy of the particular language which has become the medium of expression for their society. It is quite an illusion to imagine that one adjusts to reality essentially without the use of language and that language is merely an incidental means of solving specific problems of communication or reflection. The fact of the matter is that the 'real world' is to a large extent built up on the language habits of the group. No two languages are ever sufficiently similar to be considered as representing the same social reality ... We see and hear and otherwise experience very largely as we do because the language habits of our community predispose certain choices of interpretation.
>
> ('The Status of Linguistics as a Science' in *Essays on Culture, Language and Personality*)

In short, for the Talking Animal, culture and language are so intimately connected that 'way of life' is all but inextricable from way of speaking.

Of course, 'ways of speaking' differ, and B. L. Whorf was one of the first linguists to suggest that man's experience of life is in fact conditioned to a significant extent by the nature of the particular language he speaks, and in whose terms he apprehends the world. Each language, Whorf argued (perhaps echoing Giambattista Vico), formulates experience in its own way, by means of its own structure, and is 'not merely a reproducing instrument for voicing ideas, but rather is itself the shaper of ideas, the program and guide for the individual's mental activity, for his analysis of impressions, for his synthesis of his mental stock in trade' (*Language, Thought and Reality*, pp. 57 ff.). Thus the speaker of *Hopi* (an American Indian language) 'sees the world' through the lens of his own language, and that world differs significantly from the one seen by the native speaker of English.

Serious objections to Whorf's arguments are possible, and have been made. Nevertheless, other anthropologists confirm the general principle involved. Emile Durkheim, for example, puts the case that

> Language, and consequently the system of concepts which it translates, is the product of a collective elaboration. What it expresses is the manner in which society as a whole represents the facts of experience.
>
> (quoted in Herbert Landar, *Language and Culture*, p. 149)

In fact, simple observation forces us to recognize, as Franz Boas points out, that the 'facts of experience' can be differently classified, and so in one way be differently 'experienced' by speakers of different languages:

> The classification of experience which is the foundation of linguistic expression does not follow the same principles in all American languages. On the contrary, many different forms are found. The content of nouns and of verbs depends on cultural conditions. What for a

people of temperate zone is simply 'ice' has many shades of meaning for an Arctic people like the Eskimo, 'salt-water ice, fresh-water ice, drifting ice, ice several years old'. Terms of relationship and those relating to social structure vary in their contents; classifications occur such as animate and inanimate; long, flat, or round; female and non-female. In verbs modalities of action, forms of object acting or acted upon, or local ideas may be expressed. In short, the variety of linguistic content is very great.

(quoted in Landar, *op. cit.*, p. 151)

On one level, all this is self-evidently true. Each culture obviously has words by means of which it can refer to the objects which confront it; hence the *vocabulary* of a language reflects faithfully the material aspects of its culture. A group of people who had never had the experience of seeing or hearing of a refrigerator would be compelled to invent or borrow a suitable word when they were introduced to one, and would have to find a way of including that word in the language.

On another level, what applies to *things* could also be said to apply to *concepts* and *categories* of thought. 'Language', Durkheim said, 'is not merely the external covering of a thought; it is also its internal framework. It does not confine itself to expressing the thought after it has once been formed; it also aids in making it' (quoted in Landar, *op. cit.*, p. 230).

When we look at non-European languages this point is strikingly made. The English language contains a concept such as the range of colours in a spectrum which it expresses by means of discrete categories, *red, orange, yellow, green, blue, purple* and so on. This constitutes part of our culture in the sense that we as English speakers think and act, in respect of colour, in terms of such categorization. However, in a language like *Bassa* (a language of Liberia) the range of colours in the same spectrum is divided into only two major categories (see H. A. Gleason, *An Introduction to Descriptive Linguistics*, pp. 4–5).

Now whilst it may be tempting to infer that the *Bassa* speaker is in some way 'less civilized' than we, or even that his sight is defective, such explanations of this phenomenon are plainly naïve. The facts of the matter indicate that the Bassa speaker sees exactly what we see, but that for our words *purple, blue,* and *green* he says one word, and for *red, orange* and *yellow* he says another. That the difference in categories here must be of social and conventional origin, that is, a cultural as well as a linguistic one, can be readily seen when we recognize that the categorization employed by *both* languages is in any case quite arbitrary. 'Colour' is a continuum, and if *six* colours exist in the spectrum, why not sixty-six or six million and six? (A scientist might tell us that no two 'yellows' are the same, for example.) It is not that we English speakers are right and that the *Bassa* speaker is not, but simply that both our languages classify colour into quite arbitrary categories. We do so, as Boas argues, because these categories are the ones that are congruent with the nature of our particular culture.

If we accept therefore that the language provides a faithful mirror of the culture in the largest conceptual sense, we should also accept that most aspects of the culture will also find some representation in the language in terms of vocabulary, syntax, and metaphor. This means simply that we are able to talk fully, in English, about whatever we do and think as members of an English culture, which is obviously true. Equally obvious is the fact that it would be difficult to talk as fully in English about non-English cultures, or as fully in a language other than English about the English culture. In this sense the English language *is* the English culture for practical (that is, English) purposes.

Of course, a statement as stark as that needs qualification, but its central assertion remains valid. There is an 'outside world' beyond our bodies which we call real: there are 'brute facts' that one bumps into. But we perceive these 'realities' through the spectacles of our languages, and there is no other way of perceiving them. Since there are no languageless people, each culture deals with the world, reaches it in fact, through its own linguistic structures, and it can hardly avoid imposing these on reality. And the 'brute facts' of life tend to appear in different guises and call forth different responses in different cultures. As Margaret Mead puts it (*Male and Female*, pp. 54 ff.) the metaphor we may embody in a simple statement such as 'Love will find a way' may simply not exist in some cultures, or may have an utterly different role (and so call forth appropriately different responses) in others. Hence in some languages it just would not be possible to make such a statement without indicating that it was a bizarre and foreign notion. In fact English contains, as overt 'ways of putting' things, covert metaphorical presuppositions about the nature of the 'reality' outside us which clash glaringly with the way in which other peoples perceive it. As Dorothy Lee found, an analysis of an Indian language like *Wintu* throws the matter into relief:

> Recurring through all this is the attitude of humility and respect toward reality, toward nature and society. I cannot find an adequate English term to apply to a habit of thought that is so alien to our culture. We are aggressive toward reality. We say, This is bread; we do not say, as the Wintu, *I call this bread* or *I feel* or *taste* or *see it to be bread.* The Wintu never says starkly *this is*; if he speaks of reality that is not within his own restricting experience, he does not affirm it, he only implies it. If he speaks of his experience he does not express it as categorically true.
>
> ('Linguistic Reflection of Wintu Thought')

Whorf has argued that English contains metaphorical devices in its 'grammar' which impose a system of spatial and temporal relationships on objects and events (and these are part of 'brute fact' for us) which other languages, and other cultures, do not (*Language, Thought and Reality*, pp. 134 ff.). Our tense system for example, imprints a dimension of past, present, and future on our experience, which other languages (which do not by any means share a remotely similar system of tenses) take no account of. Our metaphors also unconsciously reflect a particular 'reality'. We speak of 'reaching' a 'point', 'coming to' or 'drawing' a conclusion, 'higher' education, without recognizing the implicit linear notions of movement, along a graduated path or 'up' a scale and 'towards' a 'goal', which these and similar structures metaphorically presuppose. And yet these presuppositions affect our lives as part of a 'reality' which exists, concretely, 'brutally' and 'out there' beyond us. But it is not a question, ultimately, of there being different 'realities'. What is at issue is the existence of different perceptions of the *same* reality brought about ultimately by differences in metaphor. Dorothy Lee puts it well;

> . . . a member of a given society – who, of course, codifies experienced reality through the use of the specific language and other patterned behaviour characteristic of his culture – can actually grasp reality only as it is presented to him in this code. The assumption is not that reality itself is relative but that it is differently punctuated and categorized, by participants of different cultures, or that different aspects of it are noticed by, or presented to, them.
>
> ('Lineal and Nonlineal Codifications of Reality')

In his book *The Savage Mind*, Claude Lévi-Strauss suggests the term *bricolage* as an account of the means by which the non-literate, non-technological mind of so-called 'primitive' man responds to the world around him. Using terms we have already encountered in connection with Coleridge, he argues that the process constitutes a 'science of the concrete' (as opposed to the 'civilised' science of the 'abstract') which carefully and precisely orders, classifies and arranges into structures (i.e. myths) the *minutiae* of the physical world in all their profusion. The myth-structures, 'improvised' or 'made-up' (these are rough translations of the process of *bricoler*) as *ad hoc* responses to an environment, then serve to establish analogies between the ordering of nature and that of society, and so satisfactorily 'explain' the world and make it able to be lived in. 'Nature' and 'culture' are thus caused to mirror each other.

A significant feature of *bricolage* is the ease with which it enables the non-civilized *bricoleur* to establish satisfactory *metaphorical* relationships between his own life and the life of nature instantaneously and without puzzlement or hesitation;

> The mythical system and the modes of representation it employs serve to establish homologies between natural and social conditions or, more accurately, it makes it possible to equate significant contrasts found on different planes: the geographical, meteorological, zoological, botanical, technical, economic, social, ritual, religious and philosophical.
>
> *(The Savage Mind*, p. 93)

In other words, the 'savage' mind has its own 'socio-logic' which operates by means of an immense number of possible metaphorical 'transformations' in a 'totemic' mode (the totem providing the means of transcending the oppositions between nature and culture). It is a mind which is 'multi-conscious'; able and willing to respond to an environment on more than one level simultaneously, and constructing in the process an elaborate and to us a bewilderingly complex 'world picture' out of its images.

> The savage mind deepens its knowledge with the help of *imagines mundi*. It builds mental structures which facilitate an understanding of the world in as much as they resemble it. In this sense savage thought can be defined as analogical thought.
>
> *(Ibid.*, p. 263)

'Analogical thought' necessarily imposes on the world a series of contrastive 'orderings' to which all members of the culture tacitly assent. These 'orderings' are analogically related to each other. Thus, an analysis of the analogical nature of the distinctions made between the 'contrasts' of 'hot' and 'cold', 'raw' and 'cooked' and so on will provide inroads into the nature of the 'reality' that each culture perceives.

A good example is the contrast between 'edible' and 'inedible' which all cultures maintain. Obviously, the nature of the items placed under either of these two headings will crucially determine the way of life involved, since what is at stake is assent to the same 'ordering' of almost the entire natural world. So fundamental a principle is this, that cultures will not infrequently be moved to distinguish a 'foreign' culture from their own on this basis, so that the contrast 'edible-inedible' will always be analogically related to the contrast 'native-foreign'. This means that analogical 'transferences' between the two sets of contrasts become possible: 'that which is inedible' becomes analogous to 'that which is foreign'. So, one of the persistent English metaphors for the French occurs because frogs' legs, placed under the heading 'edible' in France, find themselves under the heading 'inedible' in Britain.

In effect, the point that concerns us about the relationship between all such 'orderings' of nature is that they constitute the source of metaphor – and not just amongst so-called 'primitive' people. Thus, in the Medieval-Elizabethan period in Britain, it is a commonplace that various ordered 'hierarchies' existed as part of an accepted 'Chain of Being', and that these were woven into the fabric of everyday life. The king was chief of the State, with his nobles ranged under him. The Sun was chief amongst the planets, with the other planets ranged under him. The Lion was chief amongst animals, the Head was the chief element in the body, and so on. The analogical relationship between these hierarchies then becomes, as is well-known, a basis for making metaphors. The sun is the 'royal' planet. The king reigns, as the Sun shines (the French metaphor *le roi soleil* comes from this source); the king can be called 'Lion-hearted'; he is 'head' of the 'body politic' and so on. The best-known example is probably the metaphors in this speech of Ulysses, from Shakespeare's *Troilus and Cressida*:

> The heavens themselves, the planets, and this centre,
> Observe degree, priority and place,
> Insisture, course, proportion, season, form,
> Office and custom, in all line of order:
> And therefore is the glorious planet Sol
> In noble eminence enthroned and sphered
> Amidst the other; whose medicinable eye
> Corrects the ill aspects of planets evil,
> And posts, like the commandment of a king,
> Sans check, to good and bad . . .
>
> (I, iii, 85–94)

In a sense, of course, metaphors of such a sort had a 'formal' status in the society. They were 'officially' approved, even designated, by the political and theological philosophies of the time. Nevertheless, the process of *bricolage*, the establishment of 'homologies between natural and social conditions' natural to the 'savage mind' is clearly discernible in them.

But let us look at an informal, 'unofficial' example, which in fact shows the underlying contrastive principle strongly at work. All cultures distinguish between concepts such as 'high' and 'low', 'up' and 'down', 'quick' and 'slow', and impose these distinctions on nature at large. In general terms, in Britain, Western Europe and America, birds such as the eagle would be placed under 'high' and 'up' and 'quick', and snails and other similar creatures under 'low' and 'down' and 'slow'. We could then construct metaphors in which the 'transference' involved those qualities:

> . . . the gallant monarch is in arms,
> And like an eagle o'er his aery towers
> To souse annoyance that comes near his nest.
>
> (Shakespeare, *King John*)

> Yet he looks he like a King, behold his eye,
> As bright as is the eagle's, lightens forth
> Controlling majesty.
>
> (Shakespeare, *Richard II*)

Then the whining schoolboy with his satchel
And shining morning face, creeping like snail
Unwillingly to school.

(Shakespeare, *As You Like It*)

Such metaphors, if not particularly exciting, seem 'natural' to us. However, what emerges from the work of anthropologists like Lévi-Strauss is the extent to which these metaphors are *relative* in their validity to the 'way of life' from which they spring. They are, in short, culturally determined; effectively 'limited' to those cultures which share the particular 'ordering' of nature which is at stake.

This is not to say that there are groups of people who think that eagles do not fly high, quickly, or that snails do not move along the ground, slowly. But there are cultures which give a more complex role to these creatures and find different sorts of significance in other aspects of them.

Lévi-Strauss tells, for example, of the American Indian tribe, the Hidatsa, for whom eagles are very special birds, and to hunt them a sacred pursuit. The difficult task of trapping a live eagle is accomplished by digging a hole in the ground, getting into it, covering the hole with brushwood, and placing pieces of meat on top of that covering. When the eagle swoops down to pick up the meat, the eagle-catcher reaches up from his hole, and grabs the eagle by the legs from beneath. Hence, *in that culture*, the eagle is involved in a very much more complex set of contrastive associations than in our own. And certain conceptual relationships derive from this situation that, quite clearly, form the basis for analogies which can resolve themselves naturally into metaphors.

For instance, the very existence of the eagle there invokes the contrast of *hunter* (man) and *hunted* (animal). Equally, the eagle can in this situation be associated as much with the *earth* (the 'low') in a complex way, as with the *sky* (the 'high'); even with the hunter's physical experience of being inside the earth (possibly as the child is inside the mother). Not only is man the *hunter*, he is also himself the *trap*, and, as Lévi-Strauss continues,

> . . . to play this part he has to go down into the pit, that is, to adopt the position of a trapped animal. He is both hunter and hunted at the same time.

(op. cit., p. 50)

And of course the hunter assumes a *low* (the 'lowest') position in order to trap a quarry which is otherwise in the *high* category (even the 'highest'; eagles not only fly high, they are at the top of the hierarchy of birds). In short, a whole way of life would invest the meaning of any 'eagle' metaphor over and above any intrinsic 'significance' its constituent parts may have, in a way that certainly does not form part of our own no less complex response to 'his eye/As bright as is the eagle's'.

And so it is possible to suggest that what we can learn from anthropology is that the 'reality' we place over the 'hurrying of material' becomes ultimately the fundamental source of our metaphors, as a result of the potential 'transference' from one 'ordering' of nature to another that is any reality's central characteristic. For it is clear that the 'way of life' of all cultures springs from the particular system of differentiations, contrasts, 'opposites' and the range of possible analogical transferences between these to which assent is tacitly and uniformly given *in the language*. As Lévi-Strauss argues,

> . . . the operative value of the systems of naming and classifying commonly called totemic derives from their formal character: they are codes suitable for conveying messages which can be transposed into other codes, and for expressing messages received by means of different codes in terms of their own system.

(op. cit., pp. 75–6)

In other words, the process is the *metaphoric* one of speaking of A as if it were B or of 'getting at' A 'through' B. To understand the *form* of the system (not its content which, as in the case of the eagle-

hunters, appears incomprehensible viewed on its own) is to understand the way of life which creates the system and thereby guaran-
tees the 'convertibility of ideas between different levels of social
reality' on which all social life, and thus all human life, depends.
Man, in short, is the 'transferring' or metaphoric animal, or he is
nothing.

What this means finally is that metaphor in all societies will have
a 'normative' and reinforcing aspect, as well as an 'exploratory'
one. It will be as much concerned with what we know as it is with
what we don't know; it will retrench and corroborate as much as
it will expand our vision. Moreover, the notion of metaphor as
some sort of 'deviation' from the norm can hardly be allowed to
stand in its simple form. In many ways, what metaphor actually
achieves will be not deviation, but confirmation.

In short, and especially as part of its 'background' function,
metaphor draws attention to and asks assent for the *minutiae* of
correspondences, analogies and contrastive 'opposites' on which
'our' world depends. It asks 'A is like B, isn't it?' and thus also
asserts by implication that 'A is the opposite of C, and B is the
opposite of D'. Like language itself, metaphor thus binds the culture together in a rough unity of experience. If a metaphor surprises us in its capacity as 'foreground' it does so often because it
points to a relationship that our way of life has already presupposed, but which has not before been 'brought out'. Metaphors
affirm, in the end, as much as they challenge. We might even con-
clude that if they seem sometimes to shake the bars of our cage, it
is often only to demonstrate how firmly, how comfortably, these
are fixed.

6

Conclusions

> In the long run the truth does not matter
>
> (Wallace Stevens)

There seem, then, to be two fundamental views of metaphor. There is what might be called the *classical* view, which sees metaphor as 'detachable' from language; a device that may be imported into language in order to achieve specific, pre-judged effects. These aid language to achieve what is seen as its major goal, the revelation of the 'reality' of a world that lies, unchanging, beyond it.

And there is what might be called the *romantic* view, which sees metaphor as inseparable from a language which is 'vitally metaphorical', and a 'reality' which is ultimately the end-product of an essentially 'metaphorical' interaction between words and the 'hurrying of material' that they encounter daily. Metaphor, deliberately invoked, intensifies language's characteristic activity, and involves, quite literally, the creation of 'new' reality.

The two notions of language presupposed by these views of metaphor perhaps represent extremes which have tended from time to time to draw poets, or groups of poets to them. Those drawn to the 'classical' view tend to think of language ideally as an instrument of clarification, and thus most effective, possibly, when committed to written form. Those drawn to the 'romantic' view tend to think of language as committed *against* one kind of clarity, in the name of another which might seem by comparison a kind of confusion. Their preference is for a language which retains the resonance and 'ambiguities' of the speaking voice. And of course there is a large middle ground between these extremes.

If there is a 'modern' view of metaphor, it is an extension of the romantic one, though with some interesting developments which suggest that the two extremes are not irrevocably opposed. There is the neo-classical linguistic approach, which recognizes the validity of the romantic view to the extent that it allows for a 'vitally metaphorical' sort of 'background' to language, but which proposes an investigation of the processes whereby metaphor may be inculcated in language as 'foreground'. And there is the neo-romantic anthropological view, which recognizes the extent to which metaphors 'create' reality for us, but which points out that it is not a new reality, so much as the reinforcement and restatement of an older one which our total way of life presupposes.

No doubt this account represents a considerable oversimplification of a most complex subject. Metaphor itself has an immediacy and a vitality that mocks at all such reductive explanations of the process. However, in the long run the 'truth' does not matter because the only access to it is by means of metaphor. The metaphors matter: they are the truth. Regrettably there is, to quote Wallace Stevens for the last time, 'no such thing as a metaphor of a metaphor'.

Select Bibliography

I. WORKS REFERRED TO

ARISTOTLE, *On The Art of Poetry*, in *Classical Literary Criticism*, trans. T. S. Dorsch, Penguin Books, 1965.
Rhetoric, trans. W. Rhys Roberts, Vol. XI of *Works*, ed. W. D. Ross, Oxford 1924.

ATKINS, J. W. H., *Literary Criticism in Antiquity*, 2 vols., Cambridge, 1934.

BARFIELD, OWEN, *Poetic Diction*, London, 1928.
'Poetic Diction and Legal Fiction', in *Essays Presented to Charles Williams*, London, 1947.

BROOKE-ROSE, CHRISTINE, *A Grammar of Metaphor*, London, 1958.

CICERO, *De Oratore*, trans. E. W. Sutton and H. Rackham, 2 vols., Loeb Classical Library, London, 1942.

COLERIDGE, SAMUEL TAYLOR, *Biographia Literaria*, ed. George Watson, Everyman's Library, 1956.
Coleridge on Shakespeare, ed. Terence Hawkes, Penguin Books, 1969.

DANTE ALIGHIERI, *The Letters of Dante*, trans. Paget Toynbee, Oxford, 1920.
The letter to Can Grande della Scala is No. X.

EMPSON, WILLIAM, *Seven Types of Ambiguity*, London, 1930; 1953.

FIRTH, J. R., *Papers in Linguistics 1943–51*, Oxford, 1957. 'Collocation' is dealt with pp. 194 ff.

GLEASON, H. A., *An Introduction to Descriptive Linguistics*, New York, 1955.

HERDER, JOHANN GOTTFRIED, *Abhandlung über den Ursprung der Sprache*, Berlin, 1772; ed. Claus Träger, Berlin, 1959.

HORACE, *On The Art of Poetry*, in *Classical Literary Criticism*, trans. T. S. Dorsch, Penguin Books, 1965.

HULME, T. E., *Speculations*, London, 1924.

JAKOBSON, ROMAN, 'Closing statement: linguistics and poetics' in T. A. Sebeok (ed.), *Style in Language*, Cambridge, Mass. M.I.T. Press, 1960 pp. 350–77.

——and HALLE, MORRIS, *Fundamentals of Language* (Janua Linguarum, Series Minor, I, The Hague, Mouton, 1956). Part II of this work, 'Two aspects of language and two types of aphasic disturbances', pp. 69–96, is by Jakobson.

JOHNSON, SAMUEL, *Lives of the English Poets*, ed. George Birkbeck Hill, Oxford, 1905.
The Rambler, ed. W. J. Bate and A. B. Strauss (The Yale Edition of Johnson's *Works*, Vols. 3–5, 1969).
Johnson on Shakespeare, ed. W. K. Wimsatt, Penguin Books, 1969.

LANDAR, HERBERT, *Language and Culture*, Oxford, 1966.

LEE, DOROTHY, 'Linguistic Reflection of Wintu Thought', *International Journal of American Linguistics*, Vol. 10, 1944.
'Lineal and Nonlineal Codifications of Reality' in Edmund Carpenter and Marshall McLuhan (eds.) *Explorations in Communication*, Boston, 1960.

LEECH, GEOFFREY N., 'Linguistics and the Figures of Rhetoric', in Roger Fowler (ed.), *Essays on Style and Language*, London, 1966.
A Linguistic Guide to English Poetry, London, 1969.

LÉVI-STRAUSS, CLAUDE, *The Savage Mind*, 1962: English translation, London, 1966.

LEVIN, SAMUEL R., *Linguistic Structures in Poetry (Janua Linguarum* series, No. XXIII, The Hague, 1962).
'Poetry and Grammaticalness', in Seymour Chatman and Samuel R. Levin (eds.), *Essays on the Language of Literature*, Boston, 1967, pp. 224–30.

LONGINUS, *On the Sublime*, in *Classical Literary Criticism*, trans. T. S. Dorsch, Penguin Books, 1965.

MCINTOSH, ANGUS, 'Patterns and Ranges', *Language*, Vol. 37, No. 3, 1961.

MCKEON, RICHARD, 'Aristotle's Conception of Language and the Arts of Language', in R. S. Crane (ed.), *Critics and Criticism, Ancient and Modern*, Chicago, 1952.

MCLUHAN, H. MARSHALL, 'The Effect of the Printed Book on Language in the 16th Century', in Edmund Carpenter and Marshall McLuhan (eds.), *Explorations in Communication*, Boston, 1960, pp. 125–35.

MEAD, MARGARET, *Male and Female*, Penguin Books, 1962.

MILLER, PERRY, *The New England Mind*, New York, 1939.

MUKAŘOVSKÝ, JAN, 'Standard Language and Poetic Language', in *A Prague School Reader on Aesthetics, Literary Structure, and Style*, selected and translated by Paul L. Garvin, Georgetown University Press, Washington D.C., 1964, pp. 17–30.
This essay is also included in the collections edited by Donald

C. Freeman, and by Chatman and Levin (see Further Reading).

MURRY, JOHN MIDDLETON, *Countries of the Mind*, Second Series, London, 1931.

NOWOTTNY, WINIFRED, *The Language Poets Use*, London, 1962.

ONG, WALTER J., *Ramus, Method, and the Decay of Dialogue*, Harvard, 1958.

PLATO, *The Dialogues*, 4 vols., trans. B. Jowett, Oxford (4th edn.) 1953.

PUTTENHAM, GEORGE, *The Arte of English Poesie* (1589), in C. Gregory Smith (ed.), *Elizabethan Critical Essays*, Oxford, 1904.

QUINTILIAN, *Institutio Oratoria*, trans. H. E. Butler, 4 vols., Loeb Classical Library, London, 1920–22.

Rhetorica ad Herennium, trans. H. Caplan, Loeb Classical Library, London, 1954.

RICHARDS, I. A., *Principles of Literary Criticism*, London, 1924, 1926.
Coleridge on Imagination, London, 1934; 3rd edn., 1962.
The Philosophy of Rhetoric, Oxford, 1936.

SAPIR, EDWARD, 'The Status of Linguistics as a Science', in *Essays on Culture, Language and Personality*, ed. David G. Mandelbaum, Berkeley, California, 1964.

SHELLEY, PERCY BYSSHE, *Defence of Poetry*, in *Prose Works*, 2 vols., ed. Richard Herne Shepherd, London, 1906, Vol. II, pp. 1–38.

SMITH, HENRY LEE, 'Introduction' to E. L. Epstein and Terence Hawkes, *Linguistics and English Prosody; Studies in Linguistics*, Occasional Paper No. 7, Buffalo N.Y., 1959.

SPRAT, THOMAS, *The History of the Royal Society of London*, London, 1667; 1702; 1722. Ed. Jackson I. Cope and Harold Whitmore Jones, Washington University, St Louis, Miss., 1959.

STEVENS, WALLACE, the quotations are all from *Adagia*, in *Opus Posthumous*, London, 1959.

TUVE, ROSEMOND, *Elizabethan and Metaphysical Imagery*, Chicago, 1947.

VICO, GIAMBATTISTA, *The New Science*, a revised translation of the third edition by Thomas Goddard Bergin and Max Harold Fisch, Cornell, 1971.

VINSAUF, GEOFFREY DE, *Poetria Nova* (c. 1210), in Edmond Faral (ed.), *Les Arts Poétiques du XIIᵉ et du XIIIᵉ siècle*, Paris, 1924.

WHEELWRIGHT, PHILIP, *The Burning Fountain*, Indiana, 1954. *Metaphor and Reality*, Indiana, 1962.

WHORF, BENJAMIN LEE, *Language, Thought and Reality*, Cambridge, Mass., 1956.

WORDSWORTH, WILLIAM, *Preface to the Lyrical Ballads* (1800 and 1802), in Wordsworth and Coleridge, *Lyrical Ballads*, edd. R. L. Brett and A. R. Jones, London, 1963.

2. SUGGESTIONS FOR FURTHER READING

The following general works contain a good deal of interesting material:

FOSS, MARTIN, *Symbol and Metaphor in Human Experience*, London, 1949.

WIMSATT, WILLIAM K. and BROOKS, CLEANTH, *Literary Criticism: a Short History*, London, 1957. Particularly good on developing attitudes towards metaphor in a social and literary context.

WELLEK, RENÉ and WARREN, AUSTIN, *Theory of Literature*, 1949, 1954, Penguin Books, 1963. Chapter 15 is on Image, Metaphor, Symbol and Myth, and there is an extensive bibliography.

PREMINGER, ALEX, WARNKE, FRANK J. and HARDISON jr., O.B. (eds.), *Encyclopedia of Poetry and Poetics*, Princeton, 1965. See particularly the articles on 'Metaphor', 'Linguistics and Poetics', 'Imagery', 'Symbol'. Excellent for browsing.

MIALL, DAVID, ed., *Metaphor: Problems and Perspectives*, Brighton, 1982.

The following works bring together some provocative material, particularly in connection with linguistic approaches to Metaphor.

SEBEOK, T. A., ed., *Style in Language*, Cambridge, Mass., M.I.T. Press, 1960. A fascinating and wide-ranging record of a conference on linguistics and literature, which contains some 'classic' statements. Well worth dipping into. On metaphor, see especially Roman Jakobson, 'Concluding Statement, Linguistics and Poetics', pp. 350–77 mentioned above.

CHATMAN, SEYMOUR and LEVIN, SAMUEL, R. (eds.), *Essays on the Language of Literature*, Boston, 1967.
See the essays by Levin and Mukařovský.

FOWLER, ROGER, ed., *Essays on Style and Language*, London, 1966.
Contains an interesting essay by Leech.

FREEMAN, DONALD C., ed., *Linguistics and Literary Style*, London, 1970.
Rather specialized, but worth perseverance. Contains Mukařovský's essay.

KNIGHTS, L. C. and COTTLE, BASIL, *Metaphor and Symbol*, London, 1960.
The record of a symposium held at the University of Bristol. Rather more traditional in approach. Contains Owen Barfield, 'The Meaning of the word "Literal"', and D. G. James, 'Metaphor and Symbol'.

LEVIN, SAMUEL R., *The Semantics of Metaphor*, Baltimore, Johns Hopkins University Press, 1977.

LODGE, DAVID, *The Modes of Modern Writing: Metaphor, Metonymy and the Typology of Modern Literature*, London, 1977.
Applies Jakobson's notions to the study of the modern novel.

REUGG, MARIA, 'Metaphor and Metonymy: the logic of Structuralist Rhetoric', in *Glyph*, Vol. 6, 1979, pp. 141-57.

DE MAN, PAUL, 'The Epistemology of Metaphor', in *Critical Inquiry*, Vol. 5, 1980, pp. 13-30.

The following special studies offer valuable explorations of the nature of metaphor in terms of the areas indicated:

Classics:

STANFORD, W. B., *Greek Metaphor*, Oxford, 1936. By now a standard work.

Philosophy:

BLACK, MAX, 'Metaphor', *Aristotelian Society Proceedings* (1954-5).

LANGER, SUSANNE, *Philosophy in a New Key*, Harvard 1942.
The 'new key' has a lot to do with metaphorical processes, such as 'symbolic transformation', and draws on a good deal of anthropological work.

TURBAYNE, COLIN MURRAY, *The Myth of Metaphor*, Yale, 1962.

NORRIS, CHRISTOPHER, *The Deconstructive Turn*, London, 1983.

Semantics:

FURBANK, P. N., *Reflections on the Word 'Image'*, London, 1970.

ULLMANN, STEPHEN, *Style in the French Novel*, Cambridge, 1957.
The Principles of Semantics, London, 1957.
Language and Style, Oxford, 1964.
See especially Chapter 9, 'The Nature of Imagery'.

Linguistics:

BARTHES, ROLAND, *Elements of Semiology*, London, 1967.
An example of French 'structuralism'. See especially Section III, 'Syntagm and System'.

FOWLER, ROGER, *The Languages of Literature*, London, 1971.
Attempts to bridge the gap between literary and linguistic studies.

UITTI, KARL D., *Linguistics and Literary Theory*, New Jersey, 1969. For specialists.

RICOEUR, PAUL, *The Rule of Metaphor: Multi-Disciplinary Studies of the Creation of Meaning in Language*, trans. R. Czerny, London, 1978.

Psychoanalysis:

LACAN, JACQUES, 'The Agency of the Letter in the Unconscious', in *Ecrits*, trans. A. Sheridan, London, 1977.
A 'post-structuralist' development of Jakobson's theory of metaphor and metonymy.

Index